Robert Antelme
Humanity, Community, Testimony

THE EUROPEAN HUMANITIES RESEARCH CENTRE

UNIVERSITY OF OXFORD

The European Humanities Research Centre of the University of Oxford organizes a range of academic activities, including conferences and workshops, and publishes scholarly works under its own imprint, LEGENDA. Within Oxford, the EHRC bridges, at the research level, the main humanities faculties: Modern Languages, English, Modern History, Classics and Philosophy, Music and Theology. The Centre stimulates interdisciplinary research collaboration throughout these subject areas and provides an Oxford base for advanced researchers in the humanities.

The Centre's publications programme focuses on making available the results of advanced research in medieval and modern languages and related interdisciplinary areas. An Editorial Board, whose members are drawn from across the British university system, covers the principal European languages. Titles currently include works on Arabic, Catalan, Chinese, English, French, German, Italian, Portuguese, Russian, Spanish and Yiddish literature. In addition, the EHRC co-publishes with the Society for French Studies, the Modern Humanities Research Association and the British Comparative Literature Association. The Centre also publishes a Special Lecture Series under the LEGENDA imprint, and a journal, *Oxford German Studies*.

Enquiries about the Centre's academic and publishing programme
should be addressed to:
Professor Martin McLaughlin, Director

Further information:
Kareni Bannister, Senior Publications Officer
European Humanities Research Centre
University of Oxford
76 Woodstock Road, Oxford OX2 6LE
enquiries@ehrc.ox.ac.uk
www.ehrc.ox.ac.uk

LEGENDA

RESEARCH MONOGRAPHS IN FRENCH STUDIES

❖

LEGENDA

EUROPEAN HUMANITIES RESEARCH CENTRE
RESEARCH MONOGRAPHS IN FRENCH STUDIES 15

Robert Antelme
Humanity, Community, Testimony

❖

MARTIN CROWLEY

LEGENDA

European Humanities Research Centre
University of Oxford
Research Monographs in French Studies 15
2003

Published for the Society for French Studies by the
European Humanities Research Centre
of the University of Oxford
47 Wellington Square
Oxford OX1 2JF

LEGENDA is the publications imprint of the
European Humanities Research Centre

ISBN 1 900755 80 7
ISSN 1466–8157

First published 2003

British Library Cataloguing in Publication Data
A CIP catalogue record for this book is available from the British Library

LEGENDA series designed by Cox Design Partnership, Witney, Oxon
Printed in Great Britain by
Information Press
Eynsham
Oxford OX8 1JJ

Chief Copy-Editor: Genevieve Hawkins

CONTENTS

❖

FOR MY PARENTS
ROD AND HILARY CROWLEY

ACKNOWLEDGEMENTS

❖

For permission to reproduce copyright material, I am grateful to Editions Gallimard. I am also grateful to Leon Rosselson for allowing me to quote his 'The World Turned Upside Down', which has been greatly on my mind and on my lips during the writing of this study. I would like to thank Queens' College, the Department of French and the University of Cambridge, for sabbatical leave and financial support which have greatly helped the writing of this book.

Of the many people who have helped me during the completion of this project, I owe an especial debt of gratitude to Monique Antelme, whose generous support has touched me deeply. I also owe particular thanks to Colin Davis, Leslie Hill (*qui est à l'origine de ce livre*) and Michel Surya. For practical, intellectual and personal support, I would like to thank Kareni Bannister, Wendy Bennett, Victoria Best, Bruno Chaouat, James Diggle, Robert Gordon, Katja Haustein, Catherine Howell, Ian James, Sarah Kay, Neil Kenny, Michael Moriarty, Ian Patterson, Kyle Rand, Kathryn Robson, Emily Tomlinson, Cathy Wardle, Ingrid Wassenaar, Carl Watkins and Emma Wilson. And I am immensely grateful to Ella Crowley, Nick Crowley and Rachel Wooller, for their constant interest in this work (albeit to different degrees) and for their sustaining love.

M. P. V. C.

ABBREVIATIONS

❖

Abbreviations are used to refer to the following:

EH Robert Antelme, *L'Espèce humaine*, édition revue et corrigée (1957) (Paris: Gallimard, Tel, 1978)

TI Robert Antelme, *Textes inédits/Sur 'L'Espèce humaine'/Essais et témoignages* (Paris: Gallimard, 1996)

All emphases are original except where otherwise stated.

The World Turned Upside Down

In 1649 to St. George's Hill
A ragged band they called the Diggers came to show the people's will.
They defied the landlords, they defied the laws.
They were the dispossessed reclaiming what was theirs.

We come in peace they said to dig and sow.
We come to work the lands in common and to make the waste ground grow.
This earth divided we will make whole
So it will be a common treasury for all.

The sin of property we do disdain.
No man has any right to buy and sell the earth for private gain.
By theft and murder they took the land,
Now everywhere the walls spring up at their command.

They make the laws to chain us well,
The clergy dazzle us with heaven or they damn us into hell.
We will not worship the God they serve,
The God of greed who feeds the rich while poor folk starve.

We work we eat together, we need no swords.
We will not bow to the masters or pay rent to the lords.
Still we are free though we are poor.
You Diggers all stand up for glory, stand up now.

From the men of property the orders came,
They sent the hired men and troopers to wipe out the Diggers' claim,
Tear down their cottages, destroy their corn.
They were dispersed but still the vision lingers on.

You poor take courage, you rich take care.
This earth was made a common treasury for everyone to share.
All things in common, all people one.
We come in peace. The orders came to cut them down.

LEON ROSSELSON

PREFACE: SURVIVALS

❖

Our culture is obsessed by ideas of survival. Trivially, we are entertained by game shows in which contestants endure more or less demanding conditions in the hope of material reward. Understandably, we are buoyed up by songs which use the lexicon of survival to recount resistance to oppression, say, or recovery from romantic disappointment. Importantly, we have begun to extend our attention to the stories of those who have undergone all kinds of ordeals, and who find themselves now in the role of survivor in relation to their own life. But our notion of survival is itself also divided. On the one hand, we remain attached to a model of survival as heroic feat; on the other, we have also begun to conceive of survival as the fragile persistence of the surpassingly weak. The trivial spectacle of pseudo-survival cannot see beyond its dilute version of the first model, of course. But survival in the significant sense is also divided along these lines. To those who have endured extreme suffering, and who claim this experience as part of a defiant self-affirmation: who are we to refuse such a claim on the grounds of qualms about its conceptual foundations? And yet it is hard to consider the heroic model of survival without realizing its painful exclusivity—not least, its exclusion of those who also suffered, but did not survive. But the respect due both to those who have survived and to those who have not means that we maintain the two models, for all their mutual contradiction.

In common with the work of many survivor-writers, Robert Antelme's *L'Espèce humaine* can, to an extent, be read according to both of these models. As a resistant and (at the time of writing his memoir) a member of the PCF, his emphasis falls partly on the political implications of his experience of first Buchenwald, then Gandersheim, then Dachau; it is possible to read this emphasis, along with his concern for the prisoners' struggle to remain human, as maintaining a kind of fraternal heroism. While such a reading can in principle be backed up by Antelme's frequent use of the term

'struggle', for example, or his references to the 'consciousness' of the
deportees, it is, overall, a reductive reading. But its possibility is there.
The sense of Antelme's testimony is, however, to define the prisoners'
struggle otherwise: as the affirmation, in and against the destitution
to which they are subjected, of a humanity understood as shared
exposure to irreducible weakness. And so the model of survival which
underpins his text is complex: as will be seen, its emphasis on fragility
has much in common for example with Blanchot's attempt (and,
following Blanchot, Derrida's) to define survival as spectral; on the
other hand, the irreducible humanity which, for Antelme, remains,
spectrally, to contest its attempted abolition, retains in his analysis a
minimum of ontological presence and ethical effectivity. This strange
position, between two versions of survival, and between his time and
ours, might tell us much about the current status of Antelme's text.

One of the aims of this study is to explore the reasons for the
contemporary prominence of *L'Espèce humaine*, first published in
1947, republished in 1949 and then, in the revised edition with which
we are most familiar, in 1957. Since his death in 1990, Antelme's
popularity among students, researchers and intellectuals within and
beyond France has increased at an astonishing rate. *L'Espèce humaine*
has become an indispensable point of reference in discussions of the
nature of testimony, while also exercising a profound (if often
unrecognized) influence on recent French approaches to such
questions as the status of the human, or the possibility of community.
While Antelme's recent popularity may in part be attributed to such
general cultural trends as a fascination with testimony of all kinds, or
an interest in the politics of the Occupation and Liberation, I will be
arguing that the pre-eminence of *L'Espèce humaine* is largely an effect
of Antelme's uncanny ability to anticipate the preoccupations and
approaches of much recent thought, while retaining enough of his
own, and his period's, specificity to ensure an intriguing degree of
relative independence. The residual ontology of Antelme's model of
survival would on this account represent the specificity which allows
him to resist simple assimilation to the concerns of our present
intellectual moment—concerns which he also, however, both
anticipates and influences.

The three areas highlighted in this study—humanity, community
and testimony—therefore between them aim to summarize this tendency, while drawing a map of Antelme's intellectual relations and
legacy which takes in not only close friends such as Blanchot or

Dionys Mascolo, but others including Rousset, Perec and Nancy. In presenting this map, I will also be seeking to emphasize the extent to which Antelme's activities exceeded the writing and publication of *L'Espèce humaine*. It is not quite the case that, as is often stated, Antelme 'wrote only one book': while it is of course true that he published no other, this view tends to neglect the various writings and interventions in which he continued to develop the insights of *L'Espèce humaine*, his action—along with that of his closest friends— guided by its lights. Antelme is a more interesting, more diverse and more actively engaged figure than we can appreciate if we simply emphasize the singularity of his extraordinary testimony.

The resonance and rigour of Antelme's thought and writings have at times produced a kind of piety on the part of his readers, the mark of a premature assimilation of his work to intellectual interests whose development he may well have influenced, but whose presuppositions are not necessarily his own. By reading Antelme with detailed attention to both his work and its contexts, this study aims to restore a sense of the specificity of this work, and so to present more accurately the particular, demanding relation he proposes to us, his belated readers.

The study is organized into three principal chapters, which treat in turn each of the three areas named in its subtitle, and two interleaved 'Readings' sections. These are designed to supplement the discussions of the main chapters, by suggesting something of the significance of Antelme to other major recent French writers, and by building connections between the chapters whose flow they also punctuate. They use a variety of approaches to the readings of Antelme by these other writers, tending sometimes towards critical engagement, some- times towards commentary. In all cases, they are intended primarily to accompany the texts they describe, which offer far more to reflections on the topics considered here than I have room to indicate. I hope that these sections might provide a different way to appreciate Antelme's status: in addition to the substantive discussions of the main chapters, they offer a constellation displaying this status dynamically, if also partially. They aim to suggest something of how Antelme has been read; and, as I will argue more than once, if this reading is not an active mobilization, then it has hardly taken place at all.

One name missing from those considered in these sections, and indeed not greatly present in this study as a whole, is that of

Marguerite Duras. And yet Duras's *La Douleur* (1985), with its eponymous diary recounting, in more or less modified form, Duras's wait for Antelme during his deportation, has been enormously influential in the recent revival of interest in *L'Espèce humaine*. Some readers may therefore be surprised by the relatively small amount of attention paid to Duras in what follows. This is not an omission but a conscious decision on my part. And there are two reasons for this. First, I have addressed the relation between Antelme's work and that of Duras elsewhere (details of these publications may be found in the Bibliography). Secondly, and more substantively: Antelme is not just an adjunct to Duras, an interesting bit of extra reading to flesh out *La Douleur*. As I hope to show in what follows, *L'Espèce humaine* is an immensely significant, and immensely rich, text in its own right; and its author was a writer, thinker and political activist whose influence on his world was, and continues to be, important. It is in fact one of the aims of this study to demonstrate the extent and subtlety of this influence. I have no desire to deny the interest and importance of *La Douleur*. But Antelme has been too much studied in this context alone. It is time for us to pay attention to the other contexts, including some of our most pressing current concerns, which are also his.

CHAPTER 1

❖

Humanity

Considering the question of why certain concentration camp testimonies have remained prominent in the years following their publication, while others have fallen from such prominence, Annette Wieviorka suggests that one feature of such works is an interest in the significance of their account for our understanding of what it is to be human.[1] *L'Espèce humaine*, whose popularity has grown enormously since its first, obscure publication in 1947, is one of Wieviorka's examples of works distinguished by such an interest. And indeed, it is plain from even the most cursory reading that the principal concern of Antelme's testimony is the implication of his experience of the camps for any subsequent conception of humanity. As we will see, this question is explored rigorously and in detail; and the conclusion which Antelme derives from his experiences—namely, that humanity is indivisible—grounds the remarkable combination of lucidity and passion which perhaps above all characterizes the tone of his text.

In 1943, at the age of 26, Antelme entered the Resistance, becoming a member of the Mouvement national des prisonniers de guerre et déportés (MNPGD) headed by François Mitterrand. In June 1944 he was arrested by the Gestapo; after initial internment at Fresnes and Compiègne, he was deported to Buchenwald. His subsequent experiences, in the work camp at Gandersheim to which he was transferred, and up to the liberation of Dachau, to which the prisoners from Gandersheim were taken as the Allies were advancing, are recounted in *L'Espèce humaine*. Weighing 38 kilos, and in contravention of the quarantine in which the camp was held, Antelme was returned clandestinely to Paris by Dionys Mascolo and Georges Beauchamp (and, possibly, Jacques Bénet), thanks to the intervention of Mitterrand. Present as French representative at the liberation of Dachau, Mitterrand had been hailed, weakly, by Antelme, lying amongst the dead and the dying. Eventually recognizing his former comrade, Mitterrand had arranged the uniforms and false papers that enabled Antelme's friends to get him out of the camp and back to Paris.[2]

Written from 1946–7, at a time when Antelme was a member of the PCF, *L'Espèce humaine* was first published by the Editions de la Cité Universelle, a tiny publishing house set up by Antelme with Mascolo and Marguerite Duras, which had already put out Edgar Morin's *L'An zéro de l'Allemagne* and an edition of Saint-Just's *Œuvres* (with an introduction by Mascolo under his Resistance pseudonym of Jean Gratien), and which would fold soon after. The text was republished in 1949, unchanged save for its publisher, which was now Robert Marin. (The 1949 edition is presented as belonging to the 'Collection La Cité Universelle', and bears the legend, 'Copyright by Editions de la Cité Universelle 1947'.)[3] Although its original appearance had not gone unnoticed, this second publication brought the text more recognition, including the award of the Prix de la Cote d'amour (in preference, amongst others, to Blanchot's *La Part du feu*); in September 1949 Jean Cayrol, writing in *Esprit*, named Antelme's testimony, along with Rousset's, as standing out from 'des témoignages pathétiques' by virtue of its desire to sketch 'la physionomie générale des Camps allemands'.[4] But it was not until 1957, at the instigation of Michel Gallimard, and with the participation of Camus, that Gallimard published the 'édition revue et corrigée' that has become the standard edition.

Given these post-war origins, it is perhaps hardly surprising that *L'Espèce humaine* (like Levi's *If This is a Man*, whose early history is strikingly similar) articulates its testimony through the humanism of its day. Were Antelme's humanism simply an example of its cultural orthodoxy, however, his text would hardly have enjoyed the more recent success it has received within an intellectual context marked, if no longer by an outright anti-humanism, at least by a nervous scepticism regarding the universalist, essentialist claims it associates with the term 'humanism'. This context—which, schematically, we could map out between such names as Derrida, Nancy, Levinas and Lyotard—has developed from a critique of these claims towards a sense that some configuration of human commonality might be a necessary correlative of an ethical commitment to alterity, or political resistance to the atomizing violence of global capital.[5] I would argue that Antelme's particular conception of the human offers a kind of delicacy which has much to say to this interest, and that this is one of the key factors in his recent prominence; but also that his position maintains something of the substance of the humanism of his immediate context. Antelme's humanity, I will argue, exceeds its post-war moment by anticipating the commitment to exposure, finitude and vulnerability which marks contemporary efforts to think beyond the opposition of humanism and anti-humanism, while also retaining a kind of ontological 'bite' which helps it maintain a resisting specificity in relation to this contemporary move. In order to present this argument, I will in this chapter set out the principal aspects of Antelme's thesis of the indivisibility of humanity, before discussing the affinities and important distinctions between Antelme's model of residual humanity and a contemporary fascination with figures of spectrality.

Indestructible

The central thesis of *L'Espèce humaine* is suggested by its title, and confirmed immediately in Antelme's 1947 'Avant-propos': there is only one human race, which is not amenable to prejudicial division on grounds of race, class and so on. This might be mistaken for a heroic hypothesis, the indivisibility of humanity implying insur-mountable strength, invincible confidence; Antelme's introduction to his testimony dispels this notion with some urgency. That humanity is unbreachable is revealed, for Antelme, by its status as irreducible residue: its strength is that of an ultimate fragility, resistant inasmuch as it can never be removed. Thus, when he discusses the struggle of the Gandersheim prisoners, it is as a kind of fragile desperation, within which the residuality of the human is disclosed: 'Le ressort de notre lutte', he writes, 'n'aura été que la revendication forcenée, et presque toujours elle-même solitaire, de rester, jusqu'au bout, des hommes' (*EH*, 11). This is not, he insists, a heroism as might be conventionally understood: the claim of the prisoners is ontological, and forceful to the extent that it is also vulnerable:

Les héros que nous connaissons, de l'histoire ou des littératures, qu'ils aient crié l'amour, la solitude, l'angoisse de l'être ou du non-être, la vengeance, qu'ils se soient dressés contre l'injustice, l'humiliation, nous ne croyons pas qu'ils aient jamais été amenés à exprimer comme seule et dernière revendication, un sentiment ultime d'appartenance à l'espèce. (p. 11)

The unbreakable unity of humanity is, therefore, a solidity grounded in a biology beyond qualification—not as exclusionary confidence, but as an encounter with a boundary which cannot be crossed precisely because it is a point of absolute exposure:

La mise en question de la qualité d'homme provoque une revendication presque biologique d'appartenance à l'espèce humaine. Elle sert ensuite à méditer sur les limites de cette espèce, sur sa distance à la 'nature' et sa relation avec elle, sur une certaine solitude de l'espèce donc, et pour finir, surtout à concevoir une vue claire de son unité indivisible. (p. 11)

It is characteristic of the delicate dialectic which marks Antelme's thought that he represents the indivisibility of humanity as a kind of fragile solitude, an identity definable only in terms of its threatened abolition. And in the clearest exposition of his main thesis, it is precisely in terms of this dialectic of vulnerability that Antelme approaches his subject.

Antelme's principal exposition of his understanding of the indivisibility of humanity is introduced *via* reference to that which is not human: the animal, the vegetable, the mineral, the elemental— dogs, trees, insects, leaves, air, water. All of this—'nature', here named without scare quotes—is presented as strikingly, distinctively healthy, luxurious, robust: 'Jamais on n'aura été aussi sensible à la santé de la nature. Jamais on n'aura été aussi près de confondre avec la toute-puissance l'arbre qui sera sûrement encore vivant demain' (p. 228). The prisoners see themselves as having all but changed places with a nature whose health they envy, whose decay resembles the luxury of another world: 'Si ressemblants aux bêtes, toute bête nous est devenue somptueuse; si semblables à toute plante pourrissante, le destin de cette plante nous paraît aussi luxueux que celui qui s'achève par la mort dans le lit' (p. 228). The prisoners are approaching the non-human, aligning themselves with it. But (and this is the essential point in Antelme's argument, this reservation cannot be stressed too strongly): this movement of approach is endless, the non-human will never be reached. Again, however: this is not a confidence, the indifference of a secure limit; Antelme carefully doubles back his syntax, to reinscribe the exposure of the human even as he affirms its unbreachability, thus: 'Nous sommes au point de ressembler à tout ce qui ne se bat que pour manger et meurt de ne pas manger, au point de nous niveler sur une autre espèce, qui ne sera jamais nôtre et vers laquelle on tend' (p. 228). Not 'mais': '*et* vers laquelle on tend'. The limits of the human are affirmed only inasmuch as they are approached, in the prisoners' vulnerability; the unambiguous unity of humanity is marked in its residuality, its all-too human finitude. 'Mais il n'y a pas d'ambiguïté, nous restons des hommes, nous ne finirons qu'en hommes' (p. 229).

Thus it is that Antelme reaches the heart of his argument. The prisoners, driven by the SS to the limits of the human, still remain human. This irreducibility, says Antelme, has two implications. First, that this experience of exposure is the very experience of the solidity of the human: 'l'on fait l'épreuve de la solidité de cette espèce, de sa fixité' (p. 229). Secondly, that from below the divisions of the everyday, the human emerges as not only irreducible, but indivisible:

Ensuite, que la variété des rapports entre les hommes, leur couleur, leurs coutumes, leur formation en classes masquent une vérité qui apparaît ici éclatante, au bord de la nature, à l'approche de nos limites: il n'y a pas des espèces humaines, il y a une espèce humaine. (p. 229)

The attempt to impose divisions upon 'l'espèce humaine' which is the rationale of the camps is thus, argues Antelme, 'le grossissement, la caricature extrême' of the 'ancien "monde véritable"' auquel nous rêvons', in which divisions of class or of race allow the discriminatory platitude, 'Ce ne sont pas des gens comme nous' (p. 229).

What is revealed by the prisoners' encounter with the limits of the human is, then, that this humanity is both irreducible and indivisible. Despite the best efforts of the SS, the prisoners cannot become other than human, precisely because this humanity is defined by weakness and destitution: 'Eh bien, ici, la bête est luxueuse, l'arbre est la divinité et nous ne pouvons devenir ni la bête ni l'arbre. Nous ne pouvons pas et les SS ne peuvent pas nous y faire aboutir' (p. 229). Confronted by the twin limits of nature and death, no substantive difference separates prisoners and SS; accordingly, 'nous sommes obligés de dire qu'il n'y a qu'une espèce humaine' (p. 230). The violence of the executioner and the vulnerability of the victim are themselves both human possibilities, and between them reveal that, for all that the victim may die, he will die as a human being; while the individual may be mortal, his humanity survives.

La pire victime ne peut faire autrement que de constater que, dans son pire exercice, la puissance du bourreau ne peut être que celle de l'homme: la puissance de meurtre. Il peut tuer un homme, mais il ne peut pas le changer en autre chose. (p. 230)

With defiant, dialectical audacity, Antelme thus claims that the SS are 'en définitive impuissants devant nous' (p. 229): they are murdering human beings as part of the attempted denial of their humanity, but this murder declares the humanity it claims to abolish.

The commandment which determines the order of the camps—'*Il ne faut pas que tu sois*'—is thus merely a 'dérisoire volonté de con' (p. 79), as the executioner has no power over the humanity he longs to destroy. As a response to this impotence, the SS attempt to instigate a complete effacement of the prisoners' remains, as if this could also efface their humanity: 'Il ne faut pas que le mort puisse nous servir de signe. Il faut que les morts disparaissent ici aussi, où il n'y a pas de crématoire. Notre mort naturelle est tolérée, comme le sommeil, comme de pisser, mais il ne faut pas qu'elle laisse de trace' (p. 97).

This humanity is, however, ineradicable: and so, 'il dépend encore de nous, de notre acharnement à vivre, qu'au moment où ils viendront de nous faire mourir ils aient la certitude d'avoir été entièrement volés' (p. 79). The desperation of the prisoner, clinging to his life however he can, is thus already, immediately, a resistance to and a refutation of the logic of the camp, inasmuch as his desitution already reveals the irreducible, residual humanity which his captors cannot destroy. Antelme is not quite reinscribing a heroism of the will: the desperation of 'notre acharnement à vivre', combined with its sad failure ('ils viendront de nous faire mourir'), makes this struggle the 'almost biological' manifestation of an irreducible species-being, not the proud activity of a moral subject. Antelme is keenly aware that to locate humanity in positive qualities or capacities is to repeat the logic of the camps, by excluding from this humanity those stripped of such qualities or capacities. Resistance must thus be thought as already manifest within the prisoners' destitution, regardless of the abilities or actions of the destitute. Accordingly,

On tremblera toujours de n'être que des tuyaux à soupe, quelque chose qu'on remplit d'eau et qui pisse beaucoup.
    Mais l'expérience de celui qui mange les épluchures est une des situations ultimes de résistance. (p. 101)

'Plus on est contesté en tant qu'homme par le SS, plus on a de chances d'être confirmé comme tel' (p. 101). In a kind of historical irony (which, in the Marxist context of its composition, resonates with Hegel's 'master–slave' dialectic, Feuerbach's species-ontology grounded in need and the subsequent outraged humanism of Marx's 1844 manuscripts), the attempts of the SS to reduce their prisoners to the sub-human have succeeded in revealing these prisoners as the very image and indestructible locus of the human.[6] Impotent before the irreducible humanity revealed in absolute exposure, the SS are driven by a logic whose very murderousness is already, according to Antelme, the mark of its inevitable failure.

As Agamben writes, therefore, this indestructibility demands that the supposed limits of the human be rethought. Asking, as the central question of both *L'Espèce humaine* and Levi's *If This is a Man*, 'What does it mean "to remain human"?', Agamben notes that, in order to address this question, 'it is necessary to withdraw the meaning of the term "man" to the point at which the very sense of the question is transformed'; for 'if one establishes a limit beyond which one ceases to be human, and all or most of humankind passes beyond it, this proves not the inhumanity of human beings but, instead, the insufficiency and abstraction of the limit'.[7] During the forced march away from Gandersheim, as their captors attempt to evade the advancing Allies, the prisoners present a terrible spectacle to watching German civilians: 'On leur fait franchir les limites humaines dont ils n'ont pas l'air de pouvoir revenir' (*EH*, 254). These 'limits', however, are only those of their previous understanding of the human, as emerges when Antelme speaks to a woman, the simplest of words, no more than 'Bitte?': 'je comprends bien', he writes, 'que c'est l'humain en moi qui l'a fait reculer. S'il vous plaît, dit par l'un de nous, devait résonner diaboliquement' (p. 255). Inconceivable even as it is revealed, the irreducibly human is shocking in its very resistance.

This, then, is how Antelme configures the human: as an irreducible, resisting residue. As has been apparent at various times in this discussion of his position, this configuration is clearly dialectical: it is within and against its attempted abolition that the human is disclosed. Antelme's is, however, a dialectic without transcendence: the humanity revealed within and against the attempt to negate it neither surpasses this attempt, nor suppresses it while preserving it. Rather, the human as irreducible residue is already, immediately, the contestation of its supposed negation, a moment of immanent refusal which is a locus of value to the precise extent that it continues to inhabit the suffering it also denounces.

This dynamic also, however, necessitates the inclusion of this very negation within any subsequent definition of the human. Antelme's thesis fully implies that brutality constitutes part of what it means to be human; indeed, as seen above, the affirmation that the power of the SS is a human power, namely the power of murder, is made as part of the key elaboration of Antelme's principal thesis. Moreover, while they are not dwelt on in his testimony, Antelme does not shy away from the ramifications of this, in *L'Espèce humaine* and elsewhere (most especially the 1945 piece 'Vengeance?': see *TI*, 17–24). This dimension to his thought is best encapsulated in the paradoxical argument that part of what is proper to the human is the denial of any common humanity; this position is principally of interest for its potential to render any attempt to deny a shared humanity invalid from the outset, since such an attempt merely repeats a well-established human tendency, thereby embracing its exponent within the commonality from which he wishes to distinguish himself.[8]

It should be remembered, however, that this argument constitutes only part of Antelme's thesis; and two criticisms may be put forward of the decision to prioritize this dimension. In the first place, the would-be murderer is free to proceed with his justificatory dehumanization, since the victim, by failing to display the tendency to deny a common humanity, is, by this argument, confirming his own sub-humanity. Secondly, and consequently, the contestatory force of this argument can easily collapse back into an apparently naturalizing observation of 'man's inhumanity to man'. Nothing is further from Antelme's thought than the conservatism of this pseudo-lament; in order to avoid this collapse, what must be maintained—and what is lost in the comfort of paradoxical formulations—is Antelme's dialectic.

Formulated solely as paradox, the argument that it is 'inhumanity' that is properly human achieves a kind of ethical stasis, the blockage of paradox sliding almost imperceptibly into quietist essentialism. But Antelme's thought is anything but static, least of all ethically: it is a thought of contradiction, mobilization and outrage. For Antelme, the move to deny the humanity of the victim does not in itself affirm this humanity: rather, this affirmation is produced dynamically, in the irresolvable encounter between the desire for annihilation and the irreducible humanity which this desire discloses as its own defeat. This is why the humanity of the apparently 'inhuman' constitutes a part of Antelme's thesis: it is a necessary element in the development of the scenario which, as a whole, allows the presentation of his position. The 'inhuman' is of significance to the precise extent that it meets with an immovable resistance, in the broken form of the human.

Antelme's thought thus possesses a mobility, a development, which, as in this example, mark it as dialectical. But it is perhaps worth clarifying precisely how this term is to be understood here, and what exactly is at stake in what I have called Antelme's 'dialectic without transcendence'. Above all else, what makes Antelme's thought both appealing to and irreducible to the twin moments of its initial elaboration and its current reception is the appropriately dual need to distinguish it both from what we might see as a standard, post-Hegelian dialectic (in which the negation of the negation produces something new), and from the more recent suspicion of this model's tendency to suppress its constitutive moments of non-identity (a suspicion best exemplified in Adorno's *Negative Dialectics*, but found also in Blanchot's suggestions that the dialectic is always accompanied and interrupted by the inassimilable impasses of the neuter).[9] On the one hand, Antelme's thought involves a kind of outcome, and so is dialectical; on the other, this outcome is barely thinkable as such, and this thought therefore barely dialectical. This may be seen by a further exposition of Antelme's approach to the human.

The project of the SS is to negate the humanity of their victims. This project reveals that this humanity is irreducible. The negation is therefore negated; the dialectic is in train. But what is produced in this negation of the negation is nothing new or transcendent: as we have seen, this irreducible humanity represents the refusal of the order which has revealed it. The positive outcome is thereby inscribed within the first negation, as its immanent rejection.

In Antelme's thought, then, there is a dynamism, and an outcome. There is, thus, a dialectic, and one which is not doubled by impossibility and aporia. But this outcome is utterly minimal, and structurally inseparable from the negativity it also denounces. There is, thus, no transcendence. It is important, to understand this thought, to grasp that it is a form of dialectic, but minimally so. Dialectical, that is, to move beyond blockage, paradox and ethical stasis; minimally so, to maintain the fragility at the heart of its resistance. Dialectical, just.

Thus it is that the suffering humanity of the prisoners becomes its own immanent contestation. 'Non parce que les malheureux sont les plus forts, non pas non plus parce que le temps est pour nous. [...] On n'attend pas plus la libération des corps qu'on ne compte sur leur résurrection pour avoir raison. C'est maintenant, vivants et comme déchets que nos raisons triomphent' (*EH*, 94). With an angry refusal of what Agamben calls 'the conciliatory vice of every theodicy',[10] Antelme declares that 'c'est bien nous, *la pourriture*, qui sommes les vainqueurs' (p. 246): but this victory is no transcendence, not least because, as Antelme insists, the world which wins out over that of the camps is itself ordered by less extreme, but no less divisive, hierarchies of the more or less human. Irreducible to anything other than human weakness, the prisoners' exposure is the exposure of the human; refusing its attempted abolition in the here and now of its present suffering, their destitution rejects eschatological redemption, the better to declare its ragged contestation. *Ecce homo.*

But these thoughts come too late. The irreducible humanity of the victim is of little help to the victim in his present suffering. 'Mais nous ne pouvons pas faire que les SS n'existent pas ou n'aient pas existé. Ils auront brûlé des enfants, ils l'auront voulu. Nous ne pouvons pas faire qu'ils ne l'aient pas voulu' (p. 79). The irreducibility of the human is necessarily a retrospective thesis designed to render the logic of the camps untenable, and thus to contribute both to outrage at the events to which Antelme bears witness, and to challenges to future attempts to repeat this logic. For all that eschatological redemption is rejected by Antelme in the elaboration of his thesis, he therefore shares in the inevitably futural—hence belated—dimension to all testimonies: in Antelme's image, the ashes of the victim may fertilize a future which could do justice to the indivisibility of humanity. Indeed, the disparate figure of ash captures much of the pathos of this situation: marking the absence of the cremated victim, its hope is that its fragility might be received by a nurturing future; but this hope has no certainty. The indestructibility of the human can always be ignored, forgotten or denied; the ashes of the victim can always be lost.

Hic cinis et nihil

The future has proved particularly receptive to Antelme's testimony, of course; not least because the fragility at the heart of his testimony has found a welcome home in the pathos which has marked the tone of much recent French thought. A good deal of thinking on testimony, the human, survival, has been motivated by an admirable sensitivity to privilege, in both its objects and its own methodology, a kind of delicacy, as if to compensate (inadequately, and belatedly) for the aggressions which have made it necessary. And in this context, which speaks habitually (and at its best carefully) of ashes, of ghosts, of figures which mark the uncertainty of survival by considering the limits of the mortal, Antelme's fragile, impassioned writing has found a responsive home.

As ever, though, Antelme sits a little uneasily in this late context. For the languages of ashes and ghosts often seek to displace ontology as first philosophy, opening the space of the wholly other, irrecuperable within the being which is always mine; and Antelme, while he has little in common with the literal self-centredness which might (more or less fairly) be associated with the existentialist humanism of his day, does maintain a kind of ontology. It is, of course, a residual ontology; but, if we are to be rigorous, it will be necessary to mark the extent to which this residuality is not—quite—that which has more recently served to unwork ontological substance. It is also the case that Antelme's welcome by this later context has much to justify it, and that there is much in and around his texts which does indeed chime with the 'hauntology'—the word is Derrida's, and will be discussed below—of this moment. In the following section, then, I will attempt to assess Antelme's relation to this belated context. First, I will discuss his own use of an imagery of spectrality in relation to survival, and compare this to the more recent development of this imagery by Blanchot and Derrida; subsequently, I will explore the related figure of ash in Derrida and Antelme. While these comparisons will, I hope, give a further sense of the specificity of Antelme's approach, I will also be suggesting that his relation to this contemporary context (whose interests he anticipates, but to which he is not entirely assimilable) offers a clear instance of the combination of distance and proximity which may be partly responsible for his current prominence.

The indestructibility of the human is itself already a kind of spectrality: as noted above, it is of little practical help to 'celui qui sera cendre tout à l'heure' (*EH*, 79), but rather represents his humanity, living on without him. As Agamben writes, 'The human being is the one who can survive the human being'.[11] Just as the ghost is by definition a presence which is not present, the presence of an absence, and so on, and consequently cannot be accommodated within the realm of being, so is the human indestructible precisely because it is also subject to destruction, that which survives once it has supposedly been put to death: 'l'indestructible qui peut être détruit', as Blanchot phrases it.[12] The prisoners, Antelme claims, are beyond the grasp of their captors: 'Leur injure ne peut pas nous atteindre, pas plus qu'ils ne peuvent saisir le cauchemar que nous sommes dans leur tête' (p. 57); the impossibility of annihilation means that the murderer (like Sade's Braschi, fantasizing an impossible second death of total destruction) cannot but be haunted by the undead humanity of his victim.[13] 'Sans cesse nié, on est encore là' (*EH*, 57).

The figure of the ghost is rarely used by Antelme in *L'Espèce humaine.* He does at one point describe Jacques as 'un fantôme d'os', who frightens his comrades by embodying what they are about to become (p. 93); otherwise, he seems to resist this image. I will discuss the possible reasons for this below; for now, we might just note that Antelme seems to have reserved what ghostly imagery he does use for his writing about his own experience of survival, which is not often to the fore in *L'Espèce humaine.* In this, he joins other survivor-writers, such as Charlotte Delbo or Jorge Semprun, who have also used this image to address the strange and terrible situation with which they find themselves confronted.[14] It may be, then, that this rhetoric of spectrality also has some purchase on the phenomenology of survival as experience. Antelme's principal expression of his experience of survival (and, perhaps because of this, his principal use of a lexicon of spectrality) is to be found in his letter to Mascolo of 21 June 1945, reproduced and glossed in Mascolo's *Autour d'un effort de mémoire.*

In this letter, Antelme considers his survival, his return, and most particularly the necessity of as it were coinciding with his former self. He presents himself as located somewhere in the gap between this former self and its return, and expresses his anxiety (at the very least) in the face of what might be thought to be a reassuring 'rebirth'. This indeterminate situation clearly recalls that of the ghost, and Antelme underscores this association. Acknowledging that others might have thought of his compulsion to recount everything of his experience of the camps as a kind of hell, he writes:

Eh bien, dans ce qui chez d'autres représentait pour moi l'enfer, tout dire, c'est là que j'ai vécu mon paradis; car il faut que tu saches bien D., que pendant les premiers jours où j'étais dans mon lit et où je vous ai parlé, à toi et à Marguerite surtout, je n'étais pas un homme de la terre. J'insiste sur ce fait qui me hante rétrospectivement.[15]

Unearthly and haunted, Antelme describes himself as a kind of 'nouveau vivant', 'un appendice qui se développe' (p. 15); observing that 'je recommence à me ressembler', he remarks, 'j'ai d'ailleurs une crainte, je dirai presque, une horreur de rentrer dans cette coquille' (p. 16). This reflection concludes with an astonishing phrase, which chimes uncannily with the concerns motivating the current 'haunto-logical' fascination with the ghostly: 'Tous mes amis m'accablent avec une satisfaction pleine de bonté, de ma ressemblance avec moi-même, et il me semble que je vis à l'envers le "Portrait de Dorian Gray". Il m'est arrivé l'aventure extraordinaire de pouvoir me préférer autre' (pp. 16–17). Like the mourner anticipating the gradual dissipation of his grief, Antelme acknowledges that, with time, the proximity to his former experiences—and, especially, to their narration—which he here valorizes will diminish; like the melancholic, however, he accepts this process on the understanding that it will be incomplete, creating a haunting internal non-coincidence which, invisible, will continue to mark the otherness he celebrates: 'Il me reste encore parfois un sentiment trop vif de l'horreur mais sans doute bientôt tout cela sera-t-il aplani, neutralisé. Alors peut-être j'accepterai la ressemblance avec moi-même parce que je saurai qu'elle n'est pas; j'accepterai le portrait; il n'y aura plus de portrait' (p. 17).

Others around Antelme at this time add to this picture. Rousset, for example, refers to 'Robert Antelme [...] qui revint comme un fantôme'.[16] And Mascolo's commentary to Antelme's letter confirms repeatedly, and thematizes explicitly, his use of spectral imagery. Describing his initial period of critical illness on his return to Paris as 'trois semaines entre la vie et la mort', he also describes Antelme as 'réellement d'outre-tombe', defined by an encounter not so much with death as with 'ce qui de la mort peut être rapporté'.[17] It appears, then, that Antelme's suggestion of his occupation as survivor of a kind of limbo—and, crucially, of his preference for this limbo—at the very least anticipates the influential, spectral terms in which survival will come to be discussed by, principally, Blanchot and Derrida. Having explored Antelme's own brief use of quasi-spectral imagery, I will now spend a little time setting out the terms of this latter-day 'hauntology', in order to determine to what extent this proximity has contributed to Antelme's recent prominence.

The thinking of survival which dominates in this milieu is that inaugurated by Blanchot in *Le Pas au-delà*, and subsequently developed by Derrida. Blanchot's extremely dense definition of survival runs thus: 'Survivre: non pas vivre ou, ne vivant pas, se maintenir, sans vie, dans un état de pur supplément, mouvement de suppléance à la vie, mais plutôt arrêter le mourir, arrêt qui ne l'arrête pas, le faisant au contraire *durer*.'[18] Recalling with this vocabulary his own *L'Arrêt de mort*, Blanchot uses an elegantly confusing syntax to import into his definition the trouble it thematizes: coming to the comma after 'à la vie', one might feel this was the end of the definition: it transpires, however, that this was just the ghost of a definition, this is what survival is not (although, having been evoked in this way, this sense cannot but hang around), and the (non-)truth of survival turns out to be the empty duration of 'le mourir', itself the endless non-event of death. Derrida (implicit here in the reference to 'supplément', Blanchot's spectral 'mourir' having all the indeterminacy of a Derridean supplement, anything but 'pure') glosses this definition as follows: 'Ce *durer* insiste *sur* le *sur* d'un survivre qui supporte toute l'énigme de cette logique du supplément. Survivance et revenance. Le survivre déborde à la fois le vivre et le mourir, les suppléant l'un et l'autre d'un sursaut et d'un sursis, arrêtant la mort et la vie à la fois.'[19] Later, Derrida begins to suggest how this way of thinking survival will drift towards the spectral, in terms which might recall for us Antelme's embrace of his indeterminate (non-)position between two versions of himself: 'Survivre ne s'oppose pas à vivre, pas plus que cela ne s'identifie à vivre. Le rapport est autre, autre que l'identité, autre que la différence de distinction, indécis, ou, en un sens très rigoureux, "vague", évasif, évasé, comme on le dirait d'un bord ou de ses parages' (p. 179). And this spectrality is not slow in making its presence felt: 'Cette survivance est aussi une revenance spectrale (le survivant est toujours un fantôme)' (p. 182). This, in fact, would be as it were the origin of all our contemporary ghosts, the first boding forth of a 'hauntology' which, we must remember, is first elaborated, here, in relation to the thematics of survival.

Derrida's most extensive elaboration of the spectral comes, as one might expect, in his *Spectres de Marx*, in which its disturbing relation to presence is made explicit:

S'il y a quelque chose comme de la spectralité, il y a des raisons de douter de cet ordre rassurant des présents, et surtout de la frontière entre le présent, la réalité actuelle ou présente et tout ce qu'on peut lui opposer: l'absence, la non-présence, l'ineffectivité, l'inactualité, la virtualité ou même le simulacre en général, etc.[20]

The ghost is thus disruptive of ontology (whose job is to police this very frontier), imposing instead what Derrida dubs, 'par économie plutôt que pour faire un mot, l'*hantologie*' (p. 89). That the ghost is neither present nor absent means that it must, to an extent, be embodied: something must appear, which is neither something nor nothing. It is in considering this aspect of the ghost that Derrida comes closest in this analysis to evoking the question of the survivor: 'Car il n'y a pas de fantôme, il n'y a jamais de devenir-spectre de l'esprit sans au moins une apparence de chair, dans un espace de visibilité invisible, comme dis-paraître d'une apparition. Pour qu'il y ait du fantôme, il faut un retour au corps, mais à un corps plus abstrait que jamais' (p. 202). We might read this as analogous to Antelme's situation between the past and the future presence of his former self, internally displaced from a body which, while looking like him, is nonetheless not his likeness. 'Un rien qui *prend corps*' (p. 223): Derrida's ghost is also Antelme's hollowed survivor.[21]

The dismantling of presence operated by the ghost is also, for Derrida, a dismantling of the present, which begins to fly apart into the emptiness of the future, the time of ungovernable inheritance, the possibility of radical dispersal. 'Maintenir ensemble ce qui ne tient pas ensemble [...]', he writes, 'cela ne peut se penser, nous y reviendrons comme à la spectralité du spectre, que dans un temps du présent dis-loqué, à la jointure d'un temps radicalement dis-joint, sans conjonction assurée' (pp. 41–2). The reference is, as throughout *Spectres de Marx*, to the ghost of Hamlet's father; the undone time of hauntology is also, for Derrida, the future of testimony, a time of risk, of unpredictable emptiness. Most frequently, this time is conjured up by Derrida not by the ghost, but by a closely related figure: ash.

Throughout his discussions of Paul Celan in *Schibboleth*, Derrida suggests that the emptiness, dispersal, non-presence to which ash is by definition destined, is also the fate of the date which, explicit or not, is inscribed within any testimony. According to what is by now (1986) a well-established Derridean logic of iterability, in order to mark that which it marks, the date must be liable to return, to be reinscribed within a radically other, futural context of which it can know nothing. 'Ce qui se doit commémorer, *à la fois* rassembler et répéter, c'est dès lors, *à la fois*, l'anéantissement de la date, une sorte de rien, ou cendre.'[22] Itself, therefore, a kind of survivor or ghost, the date faces an empty future over which it has no control: 'Une date devient dès le seuil de cette survivance ou de cette revenance [...], la date de personne, le jour de personne' (pp. 66–7). Accordingly, the readability of the date is guaranteed precisely by its exposure to effacement, figured by Derrida as ash: it is 'une date qui, pour être ce qu'elle est, doit se donner à lire dans la cendre, dans le non-être de son être, ce reste sans reste qu'on appelle cendre' (p. 73).[22] Derrida's ash also outstrips all ontology, and is unthinkable in terms of presence/absence: anticipating the meditations of his *Feu la cendre*, Derrida writes:

Il y a la cendre, peut-être, mais une cendre n'est pas. Ce reste *semble* rester de ce qui fut, et qui fut présentement; il semble se nourrir ou s'abreuver à la source de l'être présent, mais il sort de l'être, il épuise d'avance l'être auquel il semble puiser. La restance du reste — la cendre, presque rien — n'est pas l'être-restant, si du moins l'on entend par là l'être-subsistant. (p. 77)

Ashes and ghosts: Derrida's figures of that which, surviving, dismantles the thought of presence, strung out between life and death, arcing towards a future of witness it can never guarantee. We have already seen Antelme's suggestion of ghostly imagery, describing his own status as survivor; if we are fully to assess his relation to this belated hauntology, then, we must first consider his use of the imagery of ashes.

Unlike ghosts, ashes regularly mark *L'Espèce humaine*. As seen above, Antelme at times steps out of his own strict testimonial situation, to weave through his account a recognition of the sufferings of those in other camps; specifically, this entails a reference to the crematoria of which, as he states explicitly, there was no example at Gandersheim. These moments generally entail an overall consideration of the significance of both concentration and extermination camps, as in the elegiac passage prompted by Antelme's memory of Good Friday in Gandersheim, with its reference to 'Toutes les cendres sur la terre d'Auschwitz' (*EH*, 195). *Contra* the Easter message of redemption, the Gospel becomes a 'Belle histoire du surhomme, ensevelie sous les tonnes de cendres d'Auschwitz'; and Christ's despair is cut through by the cries of children, echoing into the empty imagery of ashes, the always empty future of testimony:

'Mon père, pourquoi m'avez-vous...'
Hurlements des enfants que l'on étouffe. Silence des cendres épandues sur une plaine. (p. 195)

Antelme is rarely this bleak, rarely dwells this emphatically on the empty future into which all suffering may be lost. But here, his own writing already challenges this bleakness, offering in its quiet outrage some kind of future hope. And this is the tension which, for Antelme, attends the image of ashes: between dispersal and recollection, loss and hope. It may be, perhaps, that the ashes of the victims will prove fertile, giving rise to the careful reception of their resistant humanity in a future rejection of their murderers' regime:

Il ne faut pas que tu sois: une machine énorme a été montée sur cette dérisoire volonté de con. Ils ont brûlé des hommes et il y a des tonnes de cendres, ils peuvent peser par tonnes cette matière neutre. *Il ne faut pas que tu sois*, mais ils ne peuvent pas décider, à la place de celui qui sera cendre tout à l'heure, qu'il n'est pas. [...] Ils ne peuvent pas non plus enrayer l'histoire qui doit faire plus fécondes ces cendres sèches que le gras squelette du lagerführer. (p. 79)

Ash thus figures the ungraspability of the prisoners' humanity, slipping through the hands of their executioners; and also the survival of this humanity, its possible resurrection in the historical attempt to do justice to the indivisibility it marks. No more than possible, however: for the use of the figure of ash also imports a pathos which is that of Antelme's necessary uncertainty. The victim has no future, first point. His humanity may have a future—but then again. Second point. There is no way to guarantee the survival of that which survives: this is its chance (the indeterminacy that allows it to live on beyond the death of ontology), and also its fragility, its risk. Seen from the shore of presence, the indestructible human is just a ghost, in the way one would talk of the 'ghost' of a signal, nothing, no one there; the victim is dead. But: this mournful statement already allows his humanity to live on, to re-mark his human death. If the human is indestructible, then the human is indeed spectral.

The spectrality of the indestructible human is, however, itself haunted: by the ontology which returns, in Antelme's understanding, to complicate this latter-day approach. Here we see, for the first time in this study, just how Antelme sits in relation to contemporary concerns: close enough to offer a fascinating degree of anticipation, but subtly distinct—partly because he is a thinker of his time, but partly also because of the specificities of his own approach. In this case, then, Antelme proposes a model of the surviving human which does indeed anticipate recent theorizations; but he also insists, as we will see, that the residuality of humanity is not quite to be thought along the lines of a ghostly undoing of the economy of presence, a Derridean 'restance'. The something which remains does indeed, for Antelme, subsist; and so it remains, also, to disturb the language of spectral 'survivance'.

The close of L'Espèce humaine features one of its pre-eminent scenes, an encounter in the dark between Antelme and an unknown 18-year-old Russian in which, as they share a cigarette, the commonality of their surviving humanity is affirmed—not as triumph, but as fragility, exposure, pathos. For no reason, in complete ignorance of his identity, the Russian has offered this invisible stranger his cigarette; tomorrow, they will again not know each other. Antelme's summation of this delicate situation comes in one of his characteristically astonishing sentences, whose syntax turns, opens itself out to catch the tentative drama of this moment: 'Rien n'existe plus que l'homme que je ne vois pas' (p. 306). There is much here to encourage a hauntological reading: the existence of the man (here also synecdoche for the humanity he affirms) rendered uncertain by its introduction *via* 'Rien n'existe plus', suggesting he is in some sense surviving beyond the limits of existence; the dense negativity of the sentence enveloping the reader with the notion that, after a generalized disaster, this unknown, invisible shade is all that remains of humanity. This final encounter would, then, represent an openness to the advent of the wholly other beyond being, announced out of, but also irreducible to, the presence of these two survivors, whose humanity exceeds their existence. The sentence anticipates, even encourages such a reading; spectrality creeps, from both ends of the phrase, into the presence of the man at its heart, turning anthropology into hauntology by the uncertainty of survival.

It is hard not to read this sentence in this way; hard to ignore the emphasis thus created by the negative frame, 'Rien n'existe plus'/'que je ne vois pas'. But it is equally hard to remain with this reading, which suggests itself to the precise extent that it also indicates its insufficiency, its own spectral indeterminacy, the virtuality it cannot escape. For there is also an ontological reading of the phrase, as unavoidable as its ghost, in which the presence of the stranger is affirmed as presence: here, the syntax reads dialectically, the negativity of the frame itself negated by the existence of the man—in and against his invisibility, ungraspability, he is *on ne peut plus* present, he exists, here, now. And the humanity affirmed in this actual encounter is also a matter of presence, as the touch between them declares: 'Ma main s'est mise sur son épaule' (p. 306). The fragility emphasized by the hauntological reading is also important here, as its memory reminds us that this presence, this touch indeed, have no victorious strength: their triumph is that of fragility, the uncertainty of a touch over the distance of darkness, silence, ignorance.[24] But this must be thought according to the dialectical logic with which Antelme presents it: as the force of weakness, the victory of the destitute, precisely on the grounds of their misery, their irreducibly human exposure.

Thus, Antelme makes it clear (*avant la lettre*) that his model of surviving humanity is not hauntological: considering the apparent spectrality of the prisoners (in the context of his description of Jacques as a 'fantôme d'os' (p. 93)), in relation to the memory of their former individuality, he writes: 'Et parce qu'il est impossible ici de réaliser rien de cette singularité, on pourrait quelquefois se croire hors vie, dans des espèces de vacances horribles. Mais c'est une vie, notre vraie vie, nous n'avons aucune autre à vivre' (p. 92). What seems a kind of limbo, then ('des espèces de vacances horribles'), the apparent negation of anything which could be thought of as a 'life', must be thought as just that, as life, real life, here and now. The 'Mais' of this passage operates Antelme's characteristic dialectical move: if life is apparently evacuated, then this evacuation must itself be thought of as life: not to restore this life, or to transcend its evacuation, but to declare, within this evacuation, the residual presence of the life in question, as the immanent contestation of this attempted evacuation. The human survives: neither as it was, nor beyond the economy of presence, but as the residual, resisting negation of its attempted abolition. 'Merde vraie, chiottes vraies, fours vrais, cendres vraies, vraie vie d'ici' (p. 109).

Antelme, then, has an ontology: the bodies of his comrades are not the 'abstract' bodies of Derrida's ghosts, nothing made flesh:[25] they are the present bodies of the suffering, exposed to a human finitude which to be sure exceeds them, but living, existing within—as, even—this exposure. Antelme as it were puts flesh on the skeleton, thinking residuality as the irreducible subsistance of something, and that something is the human. 'Ils ne peuvent pas décider, à la place de celui qui sera cendre tout à l'heure, qu'il n'*est* pas' (p. 79; my emphasis). Rousset's full description of Antelme on his return is thus instructive: Antelme 'revint comme un fantôme, mais passionné d'être'.[26] The difference is the dialectic: Antelme's residue remains in its insistent, immediate return to challenge the order which had sought to negate it. 'C'est maintenant, vivants et comme déchets que nos raisons triomphent' (*EH*, 94).

Antelme does, as we have seen, deploy the imagery of spectrality: rarely in *L'Espèce humaine*, more so in his letter to Mascolo. More so, then, when considering his own status as survivor, than when considering his understanding of the human. Which suggests that the residual, surviving human *can*, to an extent, be figured spectrally—but that this is not how Antelme proceeds in *L'Espèce humaine*. Rather, he wishes to acknowledge here the appearance of spectrality to which he and his comrades have been reduced; but then, to insist dialectically on the revelation of the residual presence of their humanity in and against this reduction. Equally, while his use of the imagery of ashes is deeply scored by the pathos of this imagery, its fragility and dispersal,

Antelme deploys such images, on behalf of the others whose suffering they mark, to call for a protective embrace of this fragility in a future which would continue the contestation it already declares. This future cannot be other than empty, as the call is made (and this is the pathos of the ash); but it is called to become a present, and to honour this suffering by refusing its logic—at which point, the ash becomes fertile, and affirms a humanity more substantial than ghostly.

Here, then, we may observe Antelme's position between two contexts: the immediate post-war milieu in which he wrote *L'Espèce humaine*, and the contemporary intellectual framework within which his prominence has considerably increased. And what is at stake here, in part, is what we understand by the human.

Antelme is not a defiant, resolute humanist, insisting on the unbroken spirit of human dignity (even as a spirit of rebellion, as Camus would do in 1951, with *L'Homme révolté*). The situation in which the truth of humanity is disclosed—'le moment où la limite de l'asservissement des uns et la limite de la puissance des autres semblent devoir se figer dans un rapport surnaturel' (*EH*, 229)—inscribes both a vulnerability and a violence in the heart of the human which prevent any return to naïve assertions of the dignity or nobility of humanity. 'Il n'y aura pas de retour à l'ancien humanisme', writes Mascolo, and, even more definitively, considering the 'inhumanity' within and against which the human is revealed, 'Nul humanisme là'.[27] Equally, in Sarah Kofman's reading of *L'Espèce humaine*, 'la leçon des camps, aussi, c'est que la figure de l'homme y a été à jamais ébranlée'.[28] Antelme's scepticism before the messianic claims of a New Humanism (here in its Stalinist PCF guise) is, moreover, evident from an anecdote told by Claude Roy: to the declaration that 'Le Parti annonçait la naissance d'un nouvel humanisme, de l'Homme Nouveau, d'un "intellectuel de type nouveau"', Antelme replied, 'Oui, le Parti a créé un con de type nouveau'.[29]

On the other hand, Antelme does found an ontology on the unbreachable limits of the human, does assert his 'revendication presque biologique d'appartenance à l'espèce humaine' (*EH*, 11); in his terminology, it is 'l'homme' who survives. He is, therefore, a deal less uncomfortable than *nous autres modernes* with the notion of the human as some kind of locus of value. As Kofman asks, then: 'Le livre d'Antelme cautionne-t-il donc le vieil humanisme que l'on croyait bel et bien enterré?'[30]

Kofman's answer is suggested in her question: Antelme cannot be thought of as advocating a humanism—of confidence, progress, reason, the human located in positive (and therefore exclusionary) qualities—which would think to return, intact, from a world before the camps. But what other word will do, for this thinker who is nothing if not a thinker of humanity? Kofman suggests preserving, as a kind of Derridean 'paleonym', the term 'humanism', 'malgré tout ce que ce terme contient d'inacceptable pour nous aujourd'hui [...], en lui donnant un tout autre sens, en le déplaçant et en le transformant'.[31] I would suggest that this displacement might be achieved by qualifying Antelme's humanism as 'residual'. As we have seen, the human is for Antelme that something which remains within and against its attempted abolition; this residual presence is one of resistance, of the demand for a kind of justice to be done in respect of this fragile, irreducible residue.

This residual humanism offers a prime example of how Antelme bridges the gap from the time of the composition of his testimony to its latter-day reception. For its demand for justice may be heard in both contexts, albeit differently inflected. Before re-transforming it into the triumphant 'man' of *L'Homme révolté*, Camus presents a conception of the human whose residuality and force of ethical resistance bear considerable comparison with Antelme's: in his *Lettres à un ami allemand*, 'man' is 'quelque chose qui garde le sens', set against the amorality of absurdism, virtually unspecified other than as a resisting residue which calls out for rebellion against injustice.[32] And half a century later, Derrida too runs up against 'l'indéconstructibilité d'une certaine idée de la justice',[33] justice as a kind of disjointed stumbling block, incoherent other than in its cry against the evidence of injustice. Derrida, of course, tries not to thematize this residue, least of all as 'man'; Camus, working through his understanding of its resistance, will thematize it heavily, as 'human nature'.[34] Antelme is between these two, readable by both, irrecuperable within either's model, his residual humanism a call for justice in this, real, life.

Notes to Chapter 1

1. Annette Wieviorka, *Déportation et génocide* (Paris: Plon, 1992), 172.
2. These details are taken from the following sources: Robert Antelme, *Textes inédits* (Paris: Gallimard, 1996), 258–65; Dionys Mascolo, *Autour d'un effort de mémoire: Sur une lettre de Robert Antelme* (Paris: Maurice Nadeau, 1987), 46–59; Laure Adler, *Marguerite Duras* (Paris: Gallimard, 1998), 184–224.
3. Robert Antelme, *L'Espèce humaine* (1947; Paris: R. Marin, 1949).

4. Jean Cayrol, *Nuit et brouillard* suivi de: *De la mort à la vie* (Paris: Fayard, 1997), 55.

5. This interest will be discussed fully in Ch. 2 below. For now, I would cite as a few brief examples Derrida's *Spectres de Marx* and *Politiques de l'amitié*, Nancy's *La Communauté désœuvrée*, Levinas's *Humanisme de l'autre homme* and Lyotard's *L'Inhumain*.

6. Mention should also be made here of Elio Vittorini's *Conversazione in Sicilia* (1937–8), which radically appropriates a Franciscan embrace of Lady Poverty to argue that the human is to be located pre-eminently in illness, destitution and suffering. After the war, Vittorini and Antelme would become good friends; his considerable importance to the post-war political itinerary of Antelme's immediate circle is discussed further in Ch. 2 below.

7. Giorgio Agamben, *Remnants of Auschwitz: The Witness and the Archive*, trans. Daniel Heller-Roazen (New York: Zone, 1999), 58, 63.

8. In Antelme's milieu, this idea would be formulated by Vittorini in his *Uomini e no* (1945), and would later be advanced by Marguerite Duras in 'Le rêve heureux du crime', in *Outside* (1981) (Paris: P.O.L., 1984), 283–7. In relation to Antelme, it is argued through in Fethi Benslama, 'Le propre de l'homme', *TI*, 91–105; and used in passing by Mascolo (*TI*, 265). On the extent to which it should be considered an integral part of Antelme's thinking, and with particular reference to Duras's interventions, see Colin Davis, 'Antelme, Duras and the ethics of writing', *Comparative Literature Studies* 34/2 (1997), 169–83; and Martin Crowley, *Duras, Writing, and the Ethical: Making the Broken Whole* (Oxford: Oxford University Press, 2000), 163–8.

9. See Theodor W. Adorno, *Negative Dialectics* (1966), trans. E. B. Ashton (London: Routledge, 1996); Maurice Blanchot, 'La littérature et le droit à la mort', in *La Part du feu* (Paris: Gallimard, 1949), 303–45; and, on this, Leslie Hill, *Blanchot: Extreme Contemporary* (London: Routledge, 1997), 103–14.

10. Agamben, *Remnants of Auschwitz*, 20.

11. Ibid. 123.

12. 'L'Espèce humaine', in *L'Entretien infini* (Paris: Gallimard, 1969), 191–200 (192). Blanchot's responses to Antelme are discussed in 'Readings (I)' below.

13. Donatien Alphonse François, marquis de Sade, *Œuvres complètes du Marquis de Sade*, 16 vols. (Paris: Au Cercle du livre précieux, 1966–7), ix (1966), 176–7. See also Slavoj Žižek, *The Sublime Object of Ideology* (London: Verso, 1989), 134.

14. I would like to thank Kathryn Robson for her advice in relation to the following discussion, and for allowing me to read ch. 6, 'Charlotte Delbo's *Auschwitz et après*: Ghost-writing the Holocaust', of her doctoral thesis, 'Writing Wounds: The Inscription of Trauma in Post-1968 French Women's Life-Writing' (Cambridge, 2001). For Delbo's use of the imagery of spectrality to represent the experience of the survivor, see e.g. *Une connaissance inutile* (Paris: Minuit, 1970) and *Mesure de nos jours* (Paris: Minuit, 1971); for Semprun's, see especially *L'Ecriture ou la vie* (Paris: Gallimard, 1994).

15. Mascolo, *Autour d'un effort de mémoire*, 14.

16. David Rousset, *L'Univers concentrationnaire* (1946; Paris: Hachette Littératures, 1998), 183.

17. Mascolo, *Autour d'un effort de mémoire*, 59.

18. Maurice Blanchot, *Le Pas au-delà* (Paris: Gallimard, 1973), 184.

19. Jacques Derrida, *Parages* (Paris: Galilée, 1986), 153.

20. Jacques Derrida, *Spectres de Marx* (Paris: Galilée, 1993), 72. *Via* Blanchot, the signs of Antelme's influence are detectable elsewhere in *Spectres de Marx*: this is discussed in Ch. 2 below.

21. The internal void within the suffering deportee is most memorably described by Antelme in his account of 'K.': see *EH*, 178–80. This episode is analysed along the lines of Derridean hauntology, as revealing an internal non-coincidence which displaces any ontology, in Bruno Chaouat, '"La mort ne recèle pas tant de mystère": Robert Antelme's defaced humanism', in *L'Esprit Créateur* 40/1 (Spring 2000), 88–99. For an alternative reading, see Martin Crowley, 'Remaining human: Robert Antelme's *L'Espèce humaine*', in *French Studies* 56/4 (Oct. 2002), 35–46.

22. Jacques Derrida, *Schibboleth: Pour Paul Celan* (Paris: Galilée, 1986), 40. This double logic of repetition and effacement, or iterability, is first mapped by Derrida in 'Signature événement contexte', in *Marges de la philosophie* (Paris: Minuit, 1972), 365–93.

23. Recalling the debt of this hauntological thinking to Blanchot's model of survival, Derrida here deploys one of Blanchot's habitual tropes, the 'X sans X' which Derrida analyses in *Parages*; the importance of this trope to links between Derrida, Blanchot and Antelme will be discussed in Ch. 2 below.

24. The delicacy of this touch is brought out in Sarah Kofman's tremendous reading of this closing scene, in 'Les "mains" d'Antelme', *TI*, 146–51. (The initial part of this text reproduces an extract from Kofman's *Paroles suffoquées* (Paris: Galilée, 1987), 61–3.) See also the extremely astute comment of Olivier Kaeppelin: 'Avez-vous remarqué que, dans ce livre terrible, ce qui est le plus vif, le plus solide y est toujours le plus délicat?' ('L'ultime chose commune que nous possédions', in *TI*, 230–3 (232)).

25. Derrida, *Spectres de Marx*, 202, 223.

26. Rousset, *L'Univers concentrationnaire*, 183.

27. Mascolo, *Autour d'un effort de mémoire*, 37, 63.

28. Kofman, *Paroles suffoquées*, 82.

29. Claude Roy, *Nous* (1972) (Paris: Gallimard, Folio, 1980), 124.

30. Kofman, *Paroles suffoquées*, 79.

31. Ibid. 93–4.

32. Albert Camus, *Lettres à un ami allemand* (1943–5; Paris: Gallimard, Folio, 1991), 39.

33. Derrida, *Spectres de Marx*, 147.

34. See Albert Camus, *L'Homme révolté* (1951; Paris: Gallimard, Folio, 1985), 30.

Readings (I)

Blanchot

'When did *Blanchot read Antelme?' (L.H.)*

Blanchot first met Antelme around the time of *Le 14 Juillet*, the short-lived periodical established by Dionys Mascolo and Jean Schuster to oppose De Gaulle's return to power in 1958. 'Je me rappelle les circonstances', he writes:

> Je suis assis dans le bureau de D.M. (aux éditions Gallimard). La porte s'ouvre lentement, et paraît un homme de haute taille qui hésite à entrer, par politesse, sans doute pour ne pas troubler notre entretien. Il est presque timide, mais, bien plus, intimidant. Il est la simplicité même, mais aussi la réserve jusque dans la parole qui est ferme et fait autorité. Je ne dirai pas que dès alors je sais combien son amitié me sera précieuse.[1]

What Blanchot will also not say is whether, at this point, he had already read *L'Espèce humaine*, which had been republished by Gallimard the previous year. This being its third publication, and Blanchot having been on friendly terms with Mascolo since the early 1940s, it seems highly unlikely that he had not; what is certain is that his first published account of Antelme's testimony comes a few years later, after their common involvement in opposition to the war in Algeria. Blanchot's is in fact one of the first two major responses to *L'Espèce humaine* (the other being Perec's: their texts were published, respectively, in 1962 and 1963, suggesting the impetus of the Gallimard republication); this would remain the case for some time. This explicit discussion of *L'Espèce humaine* is neither the only nor, indeed, the first reference to Antelme in Blanchot's work; other such references will be discussed below. It is, however, the most extensive; and so it is here that I propose to open this account of the presence of Antelme in Blanchot's writings.

Part of a text entitled 'L'indestructible', published in the *Nouvelle Revue française* of April 1962, Blanchot's reading of *L'Espèce humaine* subsequently reappeared under the heading 'L'espèce humaine' in section V (itself now entitled 'L'indestructible') of the second part

('L'expérience-limite') of his 1969 *L'Entretien infini*. In its initial publication, it was preceded by an earlier version of what now appears in *L'Entretien infini* as 'Le rapport du troisième genre (homme sans horizon)', part of Blanchot's extended response to Levinas's *Totalité et infini*. And 'L'espèce humaine' continues to bear the marks of this provenance: its opening words ('Chaque fois que la question: "Qui est Autrui?" vient dans notre langage, je pense au livre de Robert Antelme') cite 'Le rapport du troisième genre', which dwells on precisely this question.[2]

'L'espèce humaine', then, responds to Antelme's text from a perspective influenced by Levinas's configuration of the ethical relation (as Blanchot phrases it, the 'rapport sans rapport') to the Other. For Blanchot, as we have seen, Antelme's irreducible humanity declares that 'L'homme est l'indestructible qui peut être détruit' (p. 192): as in the haunting structure of survival, the humanity of the victim exceeds its attempted abolition in his murder. Immediately, Blanchot gives this insight a Levinasian turn, arguing that this irreducibility reveals the inescapability of my obligation before this suffering other: 'nous n'avons plus aucune chance de nous voir jamais débarrassés de nous, ni de notre responsabilité' (p. 192). Recalling a key element of Antelme's analysis, Blanchot further argues that this ineradicable responsibility also reveals the impotence of the oppressor: 'maître du possible', 'il n'est pas maître de ce rapport qui ne relève pas de la maîtrise et que ne mesure pas le pouvoir: ce rapport sans rapport où se révèle "autrui"' (p. 194). This analysis echoes Blanchot's earlier exposition of the Levinasian ethical encounter, the face-to-face with 'autrui', in which 'je vois se lever [...], à partir de cette faiblesse, de cette impuissance, ce qui à la fois se livre radicalement à mon pouvoir et le récuse absolument, renversant mon plus haut pouvoir en im-possibilité' (p. 78).

This position is then developed by Blanchot into a picture of the world of the camps which, while articulated *via* this Levinasian terminology, proposes a very particular, at times even idiosyncratic analysis. The destitution of 'l'homme des camps', 'au plus près de l'impuissance', means that 'Tout le pouvoir humain est en dehors de lui, comme est en dehors de lui l'existence en première personne, la souveraineté individuelle, la parole qui dit "Je"' (p. 194). Exposed to this extreme suffering, the prisoner is abandoned—'déserté et trahi' —even by his own self ('son propre moi') (p. 194): in what appears to be an absolute opposition, 'le camp ne renferme plus qu'un enchevêtrement sans lien d'hommes Autres, un magma d'autrui face à la puissance du Moi tueur' (p. 198).

Colin Davis has rightly criticized the extent to which this interpretation obscures the struggle described within *L'Espèce humaine* to retain some purchase on the self whose dissolution Blanchot here posits as a universal, inescapable element of the prisoners' experience.[3] The analysis offered in 'L'espèce humaine' has a further dimension, however, which moves Blanchot beyond the aporia implied by his initial scenario. Possibly mindful of the third party ('le tiers') whom Levinas posits as a necessary and immediate context to the ethical relation, Blanchot supplements his supposedly evacuated prisoner with the necessity of another self, who would retain sufficient substance to be able to welcome, to shelter this devastated stranger. Noting that the failure of the oppressor does not mean a victory which could easily be thought to belong to the victim, he argues that, in addition and in response to the ineradicable ontological resistance of the victim, a further order of resistance—political resistance— is necessary: 'il faut qu'au-dehors de ce moi que j'ai cessé d'être, se restaure, dans la communauté anonyme, l'instance d'un Moi-Sujet, et non plus comme pouvoir dominateur et oppresseur dressé contre "autrui", mais comme ce qui peut accueillir l'inconnu et l'étranger; l'accueillir dans la justice d'une vraie *parole*' (p. 197). The call for justice which emanates from Antelme's account thus leads Blanchot to hypothesize the existence of one who might respond, and so to nuance his absolute opposition between the 'magma d'autrui' and the 'Moi tueur'. A whole external apparatus of struggle now becomes possible, in which this just 'Moi-Sujet' recognizes in the suffering of the prisoner 'une injustice commise contre tous', which will therefore serve as 'le point de départ d'une *revendication commune*': 'il faut que [...] le dépossédé soit non seulement accueilli comme "autrui" dans la justice de la parole, mais remis en situation de lutte dialectique, afin qu'il puisse se considérer à nouveau lui aussi comme une puissance, celle que détient l'homme de besoin et finalement le "prolétaire"' (pp. 197–8). From the abolition of the self to its return, in the instance and as the gift of the just 'Moi-Sujet', Blanchot thus moves, as does Antelme, from the destitution of the victim to the collective refusal of this oppression; from irreducible vulnerability to the collectivity this shared exposure already implies.

As I have already suggested, 'L'espèce humaine' is not Blanchot's only response to Antelme's text (although it is certainly the best known). Antelme, in fact, appears as a significant presence in a number of Blanchot's texts, sometimes explicitly cited, sometimes in the shadows of allusion. Which can only increase our sense of his importance, of course.

By 1980, when Blanchot published *L'Ecriture du désastre*, no one could be in any doubt as to his connections to Antelme. Besides 'L'espèce humaine', Blanchot and Antelme had spent the ten years from De Gaulle's return to power to May 1968 engaged in the same struggles, signing the same manifestos, agitating in the same *groupuscules*. In 1971, as if in recognition of this, Blanchot had placed Antelme's name (the final words of a piece collected under the title 'Guerre et littérature') immediately before his article 'Le refus', first published in *Le 14 Juillet* as part of the struggle against De Gaulle in 1958, around the time of their first meeting; *L'Espèce humaine* is here singled out among concentration camp testimonies as 'pour moi le plus simple, le plus pur et le plus proche de cet absolu dont il nous fait souvenir'.[4] And the publication of *L'Ecriture du désastre* itself was marked in *La Quinzaine littéraire* by reflections from Antelme, Mascolo and Maurice Nadeau (Antelme's comments are collected in *TI*, 67–8). Moreover, Blanchot's text explicitly refers to Antelme, in a discussion of the question of need which revisits and revises certain of the propositions of 'L'espèce humaine'. So the reader of Blanchot's 1980 text is, as it were, primed to hear echoes of Antelme elsewhere: and they are certainly there to be heard.

Weakness constitutes a recurrent motif in *L'Ecriture du désastre*; and it is generally accompanied by a telling epithet, as 'la faiblesse humaine'.[5] 'La faiblesse ne saurait être qu'humaine', writes Blanchot at one point, before developing his discussion, under the Levinasian sign of passivity, quite clearly in the direction of Antelme's analysis:

C'est l'irréductible-incompatible, ce qui n'est pas compatible avec l'humanité (le *genre* humain). La faiblesse humaine que même le malheur ne divulgue pas, ce qui nous transit du fait qu'à chaque instant nous appartenons au passé immémorial de notre mort — par là indestructibles en tant que toujours et infiniment détruits. L'infini de notre destruction, c'est la mesure de la passivité.[6]

Why this rapid qualification, '(le *genre* humain)'? Because passivity/weakness, as Antelme's irreducible vulnerability, is not only compatible with, it is the locus of humanity as Antelme understands it, of 'l'espèce humaine'; it is only incompatible with a humanity dreamily erected above this indivisible residue. As Agamben explains, with reference to Antelme's 'revendication presque biologique d'appartenance à l'espèce humaine' (*EH*, 11): 'It is important that Antelme uses the technical term *espèce* here instead of referring to the more familiar one of *le genre humain*. For it is a matter of biological belonging in the strict sense [...], not of a declaration of moral or political solidarity'.[7] Although, as we have seen (and will soon see again, in more detail), moral and political solidarity are for Antelme already declared within this biological indivisibility, and although the term 'l'espèce humaine' is not as technical as all that (the *Petit Robert* marks it as 'courant'), Agamben's emphasis at least helps us appreciate Blanchot's qualification, and underscores its inevitable implication: if not of 'le genre humain', this weakness is clearly that of 'l'espèce humaine', and Blanchot's parenthesis clearly intends us to make this connection.[8]

Here, then, in addition to 'L'espèce humaine', are references to Antelme from 1971 and 1980. After 1957, and the publication by Gallimard of the revised edition of *L'Espèce humaine*, it is perhaps no great surprise that Blanchot should refer to Antelme, not least given their meeting the following year. But it is also possible to find traces of Antelme elsewhere in Blanchot's writing: for example, in texts published that very year, 1957. Which perhaps suggests that Blanchot had already assimilated the sense of Antelme's testimony, and was not waiting to meet him before declaring this in his own discreet fashion.

Throughout Christophe Bident's *Maurice Blanchot: Partenaire invisible*, Antelme emerges as indissociable from a series of key moments in the evolution of Blanchot's writing. Bident's emphasis on this importance is so strong as to make the eventual meeting of the two men appear as in some sense inevitable, opening a friendship towards which Blanchot had been gravitating for some time, and which would allow him to reformulate such essential notions as the relation between refusal and affirmation. This reformulation, indeed, allows Blanchot to return in 1958 to the realm of political activity: its significance is not to be underestimated.[9] It is under the sign of affirmation, in fact, that Blanchot reprints his first published reference to Antelme, which appeared in a 1957 discussion of Simone Weil, originally entitled 'L'expérience de Simone Weil' (collected in *L'Entretien infini* under the title 'L'affirmation (le désir, le malheur)'). Blanchot refers to Antelme in a note, as confirming Weil's insight that the limits of the human condition are to be apprehended *via* an understanding of 'le malheur'.[10] This reference dates from August 1957, suggesting a familiarity with *L'Espèce humaine* which predates the Gallimard edition; Bident states that Blanchot 'probably' became aware of Antelme's text in 1950, in Robert Marin's 1949 re-publication, subsequently discussing Antelme with Louis-René des Forêts or Bataille.[11] For Bident, Antelme's influence may be noted as early as *L'Arrêt de mort* (1948), marked by, among other shadows, 'l'ombre d'Antelme, le rescapé de l'extermination'[12] (Blanchot would have known Antelme's story through Mascolo); but the principal text in which this shadowy presence may be detected is another published in 1957: *Le Dernier Homme.*

'Car Blanchot l'a lu, aimé, en fut impressionné au point de garder le silence et d'écrire *Le Dernier Homme.*'[13] But where in this text is this impression marked? The figure of a surpassing fragility, the 'last man' is linked to Thomas Mann's *Magic Mountain*, to Artaud, Beckett, Hesse, Michaux. 'De Levinas, il a la patience. D'Antelme, la pensée du malheur.'[14] And as in *L'Ecriture du désastre*, Antelme is to be found here in the disturbing effect of an absolute weakness which is also an irreducible force of resistance, an ineradicable residual presence. That this is to be understood as concerning the human is evident from Blanchot's title, where we also hear Kojève and Zarathustra.[15] That it echoes *L'Espèce humaine* is strongly suggested by such passages as the following, whose lexicon clearly anticipates that of Blanchot's 1962 essay: 'S'il était si fort, ce n'est pas qu'il fût invulnérable. Il était au contraire d'une faiblesse qui échappait à notre mesure. [...] Et surtout sa faiblesse sans mesure: c'est de cela que je n'avais pas le courage de m'approcher, fût-ce en le heurtant.'[16] The figure of what Marguerite Duras, in a text which would also be important to Blanchot, would term 'la force invincible de la faiblesse sans égale [*sic*]',[17] the last man bears the force attributed by Antelme's dialectic to the absolute victim, 'une impuissance sur laquelle maintenant nulle supériorité n'avait de prise'. Irreducible residue of an indivisible humanity—'lui, le dernier, ne serait pourtant pas le dernier'—is this the eroded subject, in need of shelter? 'Le plus infortuné et le plus pauvre des hommes [...] depuis toujours moi sans moi.' Or the just third party posited in 'L'espèce humaine', sheltering suffering? 'Quand il s'approchait, on entrait dans un espace où ce qui vous tenait à cœur était accueilli, protégé et jugé silencieusement d'une manière qui ne vous donnait pas raison, mais vous faisait espérer une sorte de justice.' Residue, in any case: 'une présence sans personne, peut-être?' Human, though? 'Non, pas encore humain, plus exposé, moins protégé et cependant plus important et plus réel.' Human, that is, as in *L'Espèce humaine*, not 'le *genre* humain'.

Il avait la faiblesse d'un homme absolument malheureux, et cette faiblesse sans mesure heurtait contre la force de cette pensée sans mesure, cette faiblesse semblait trouver toujours insuffisante cette grande pensée, et elle exigeait cela, que ce qui avait été pensé d'une manière si forte fût pensé à nouveau et repensé au niveau de l'extrême faiblesse.[18]

The last man is not just Antelme. But, like Antelme, he teaches us to re-think, to learn to think in the manner of the just 'Moi-Sujet', offering shelter to the weakness by which we are also ineradicably defined. From 'L'expérience de Simone Weil' through *Le Dernier Homme* and 'L'espèce humaine' to *L'Ecriture du désastre*, Antelme's importance to Blanchot would be just this: a rethinking of the human in terms of exposure, an insistence upon vulnerability as the punctured heart of any collectivity, which facilitates Blanchot's return to active political intervention between 1958 and 1968, and which persists after his subsequent quasi-retreat. This importance is unmistakable: as he already indicates in the footnote to his piece on Simone Weil, *L'Espèce humaine* is, for Blanchot, 'd'une signification exceptionnelle'.[19]

Kofman

He is among us, the last man: his weakness is ours, the indivisibility of utter exposure; he articulates us, is the differential interruption which also connects. 'Peut-être était-il entre nous: d'abord entre nous tous. Il ne nous séparait pas, il entretenait un certain vide que l'on ne désirait pas combler, c'était quelque chose a respecter, à aimer peut-être.'[20] The irreducibly human already maintains a commonality, mine inasmuch as it is what I still share in the puncture of my vulnerability.

From erosion, then, to a kind of solidarity, located nowhere other than in this erosion (and not its belated redemption): this is the sense of a reading of *L'Espèce humaine* which comes explicitly in response to Blanchot's, namely that offered by Sarah Kofman in her *Paroles suffoquées*. Antelme (to whom the text is dedicated, along with Kofman's father, murdered at Auschwitz) appears gradually in Kofman's study, the first part of which discusses Blanchot's early short story 'L'idylle'. (*Paroles suffoquées* is also an explicit homage to Blanchot.) This initial discussion is occasionally punctuated by a reference to Antelme (whose significance is already suggested by Kofman's title, derived from Antelme's 'Avant-propos': 'A peine commencions-nous à raconter, que nous suffoquions' (*EH*, 9)); these references soon emerge into the main body of the text, whose final five sections invert the polarity, considering *L'Espèce humaine* with reference to Blanchot.

Kofman's discussion responds to Blanchot's in 'L'espèce humaine' in part by considering the supposed reduction of those held in the camps to 'des êtres sans figure, sans "moi", anonymes, "déguisés" de façon grotesque, réduits à la pire abjection'.[21] Nuancing this reduction, she cites Antelme's account of a roll-call, his name mangled, mis-pronounced: 'Rigolade de mon nom, et je réponds "Présent!" [...] Quelqu'un s'est trouvé pour dire "oui" à ce bruit qui était bien au moins autant mon nom que j'étais moi-même, ici' (*EH*, 27). His name is no longer his name, just as he is no longer himself; and yet his name is also still his name, and he is still, in some fragile way, himself. Antelme writes 'on' more often than 'je', says Kofman: '"je" n'apparaît que rarement, souvent comme par réaction de défense, contre la "coagulation" et l'anonymat, quand Antelme décrit la perte d'identité du détenu' (*Paroles suffoquées*, 53).

The erosion of all but the residual self not only declares an irreducible humanity, it can also become the space of a common resistance. It is in its extended analysis of this resistance that Kofman's reading really moves beyond Blanchot's. She locates it partly in the shared struggle, even if conducted individually, to survive: 'D'abord les détenus ne sont pas des êtres abjects et indignes', writes Kofman; the prisoner 'n'est ni un déchet ni un rebut, même si sa seule valeur est désormais: survivre' (p. 69). The residually individual gives immediately onto the communal, and this survival is already a resistance; 'la véritable abjection n'est pas de tenter de survivre, seule manière au contraire de résister et d'objecter — c'est de renoncer à vouloir retenir "l'autre" — soi et les autres — en vie' (p. 70). Kofman quotes Antelme: 'Le véritable risque que l'on court, c'est celui de se mettre à haïr le copain d'envie, d'être trahi par la concupiscence, d'abandonner les autres' (*EH*, 101). Accordingly, resistance may also be found partly in the weak solidarity which remains possible, here and there, 'quand vous ne pouvez plus être vous-même et avez besoin d'un autre fraternel pour suppléer à votre "moi" qui ne peut plus être un "moi"' (*Paroles suffoquées*, 61).

This is, however, a poor fraternity of sufferers, in which gestures of solidarity—including the individual struggle to survive—persist only as markers of a more profound, because less active, ontological bond. Antelme's final example of such a gesture is the handshake at the end of his text, the fleeting friendship with the invisible, unknown Russian, whose grandeur Kofman signals elsewhere, in her 'Les "mains" d'Antelme'. 'Les "mains" d'Antelme? Des mains qui mettent fin à toute manipulation et à tout "apartheid"; des mains qui n'ont pas peur de se contaminer en serrant d'autres mains et ne relèvent plus d'une volonté d'emprise' (*TI*, 151).

Kofman thus connects the residual to collective resistance without passing *via* a third party quite as Blanchot had done: this resistance comes not only from the struggle to survive, not only from support given by momentarily stronger prisoners to their utterly exhausted comrades, it is also partly there within their exhaustion. After this broken foundation, 'we' are reconfigured, any subsequent ethos is subject to new demands. Commonality may no longer be thought according to shared positive identity; if we share anything, it is only— but irreducibly—our vulnerability. And so Kofman demonstrates that for Antelme there is still, in this exposure, minimally, and incompatible with any heroism, a kind of solidarity.

En montrant que le dessaisissement abject dont les déportés ont été victimes signifie l'indestructibilité de l'altérité, son caractère absolu, en instaurant la possibilité d'un 'nous' d'un nouveau genre, il fonde sans fonder, car ce 'nous' est toujours déjà défait, déstabilisé, la possibilité d'une nouvelle éthique. (p. 82)

Notes to *Readings (I)*

1. Maurice Blanchot, 'Pré-texte: Pour l'amitié', in Dionys Mascolo, *A la recherche d'un communisme de pensée* (Paris: Fourbis, 1993), 5–16 (9). Three numbers of *Le 14 Juillet* appeared in 1958 and 1959. They are reproduced in the facsimile reprint published as a special, 'hors-série' number of the journal *Lignes* (Paris: Séguier, 1990).

2. Blanchot, *L'Entretien infini*, 191, 99–100. Publication details of Blanchot's texts are given in the indispensable bibliography to Hill, *Blanchot: Extreme Contemporary*, 274–98. It is worth noting that the original versions of Blanchot's responses to *Totalité et infini* and *L'Espèce humaine* were published as three consecutive contributions to the *Nouvelle Revue française*, in Dec. 1961 ('Connaissance de l'inconnu'), Feb. 1962 ('Tenir parole'), and Apr. 1962 ('L'indestructible').

3. See Davis, 'Duras, Antelme and the ethics of writing', esp. 172–4.

4. Maurice Blanchot, 'Guerre et littérature', in *L'Amitié* (Paris: Gallimard, 1971), 128–9 (129).

5. Maurice Blanchot, *L'Ecriture du désastre* (Paris: Gallimard, 1980), 39, 52, 76.

6. Ibid. 52.

7. Agamben, *Remnants of Auschwitz*, 58.

8. Although we should note that, in his response to *L'Ecriture du désastre*, Antelme himself, defining the 'servitude' of Blanchot's thought, uses the phrase 'le genre humain jamais abandonné' (*TI*, 67). It is not (*pace* Agamben) that one term is intrinsically superior to the other, rather that the effect of the distance Blanchot takes with respect to 'le genre humain' is to underscore his proximity to *L'Espèce humaine*.

9. Christophe Bident, *Maurice Blanchot: Partenaire invisible* (Seyssel: Champ Vallon, 1998), 369–70.

10. Blanchot, *L'Entretien infini*, 175 n. 1

11. Bident, *Maurice Blanchot*, 333, 368.

12. Ibid. 293.

13. Ibid. 368.

14. Ibid. 360.

15. Leslie Hill, *Bataille, Klossowski, Blanchot: Writing at the Limit* (Oxford: Oxford University Press, 2001), 232–7.

16. Maurice Blanchot, *Le Dernier Homme* (1957; nouvelle version 1977; Paris: Gallimard, L'Imaginaire, 2001), 14.

17. Marguerite Duras, *La Maladie de la mort* (Paris: Minuit, 1981), 31.

18. Blanchot, *Le Dernier Homme*, 84, 21, 47, 27, 50, 106–7, 32.

19. Blanchot, *L'Entretien infini*, 175.

20. Blanchot, *Le Dernier Homme*, 19–20.

21. Kofman, *Paroles suffoquées*, 43.

CHAPTER 2

❖

Community

One of the principal features of French thought after 1945 is the attempt to develop a theory and a practice of community which could break with the logic seen as being in part responsible for the disasters of the war. Essentially, this entails efforts to think community as other than self-present, defined not by the exclusionary force of shared, positive attributes, practices or beliefs, but in terms of radical inclusivity, grounded impossibly in an exposure, a fragility which determine community as spaced. The members of such a community (which, in the absence of positively defined commonality, might not be thinkable as community as such) would be joined by relations of separation just as much as of connection; joined by a kind of vulnerability or poverty which would precisely not be thematizable as a bond. This approach to the question of community—and, especially, to the politics it implies —is most extensively theorized initially by Blanchot and Mascolo (influenced partly by Bataille), and then, at a later moment, by Nancy and Derrida. The proximity of such ways of thinking about community to the ideas formulated in *L'Espèce humaine* on the human as an irreducible and impossibly shared fragility may perhaps already be apparent; and Antelme is linked to these approaches by more than the shared impulse to make the logic of the concentrationary regime invalid.

This attempt to rethink community really emerges both politically and philosophically just after the 1957 Gallimard republication of *L'Espèce humaine*; the political itinerary within which this attempt is made manifest as praxis is one in which Antelme participates alongside Blanchot and Mascolo, and whose principles are affirmed by the subsequent generation. These are not coincidences. It will be clear from the names cited above that the strand of French thought referred to here is largely made up of thinkers who may be linked, more or less directly, biographically and/or intellectually, to Antelme; and I will be trying to show in this chapter that Antelme's work at least anticipates, and to an extent also influences, the thought in this area of some of the most significant French writers of the second half of the twentieth century. It will thus also be my suggestion that the popularity of *L'Espèce humaine*, over fifty years after its publication, is in part intellectually grounded in its extraordinary anticipation of perhaps the key impulse behind much of the most prominent French thought of recent years.

In this chapter, accordingly, I consider the implications of Antelme's testimony for the question of community. I address this question by first examining Antelme's discussions of the possibility of solidarity between the prisoners at Gandersheim, before exploring his membership of and painful expulsion from the PCF in the light of the model of solidarity he derives from his experiences. Subsequently, I will suggest how this model of solidarity is related to versions of community deriving from other quarters of Antelme's own Parisian intellectual milieu; this will entail a detailed return to the political itinerary mentioned above. Finally, I present some of the evidence for my claim that recent approaches to community and political organization by Nancy and Derrida are influenced, principally *via* Blanchot, but also thanks to this history of shared political engagement, by Antelme. What I would like to do here, then, is to follow Antelme's assertion that the world he describes represents the grotesque caricature of 'cet ancien "monde véritable" auquel nous rêvons' (*EH*, 229); and I propose to do this by exploring the idea that the version of solidarity he draws from his experience has a generalized significance as part of a contestation of the injustices of the world beyond the camps.

Eroded Solidarity

The title and the thesis of Antelme's memoir already imply a kind of solidarity: namely, as I have suggested, an ineradicable, ontological solidarity, the indivisibility of humanity. But this represents a very particular understanding of the notion; the ineradicable, biological solidarity implied by this indivisibility is neither comforting nor reductive, revealed as it is in the futile but no less murderous attempt to fragment it. Antelme finds unity in its utter denial; where Adorno, in *Negative Dialectics*, sees the concentration camps as having deprived the individual of even his poorest possession, namely his own death, Antelme sees in this very deprivation the possibility of affirming a humanity which the individual, dying as a human being, still shares.[1]

Antelme's central thesis is thus already marked by a kind of pathos: a connection is made to some kind of solidarity at the very moment when this solidarity is most violently denied. Antelme's thesis affirms that the sufferer is not alone; or rather, alone yet an instance of an irreducible humanity, the sufferer is bound in this suffering to a community whose virtual presence challenges the infliction of this suffering. And yet, as seen above, this affirmation is also marked with weakness: the individual sufferer is hardly helped in his present suffering by the irreducibility of his connection to the human race. The gap of suffering, which motivates the gesture of solidarity, also leaves it as just that: a gesture.

But this insufficiency cannot be simply criticized or dismissed. For it is the case, in the world described by Antelme, that positive, fraternal solidarity will not quite work. For reasons we will shortly consider, Antelme insists on this point—while also, characteristically, refusing therefore to abandon the notion. Some form of solidarity remains, in and against its supposed abolition; but this solidarity, for important reasons of inclusivity, can no longer be what it was.

In his 'Avant-propos', Antelme sets out explicitly the nature of the solidarity which was possible in Gandersheim. As part of his careful insistence on the specific features of the world he is about to describe, he emphasizes the differences between the administrative structures of different camps. In Gandersheim, this administrative structure constitutes the most important factor affecting the kind of solidarity possible among the prisoners: the fact that it was occupied entirely by the 'droit commun', to the exclusion of the 'politiques', meant, says Antelme, that collective, organized struggle against the camp hierarchy (as was possible in differently organized camps) was simply not possible here. Antelme makes a crucial distinction between Gandersheim and camps run along different lines:

Notre situation ne peut donc être assimilée à celle des détenus qui se trouvaient dans des camps ou dans des kommandos ayant pour responsables des politiques. Même lorsque ces responsables politiques, comme il est arrivé, s'étaient laissés corrompre, il était rare qu'ils n'aient pas gardé un certain sens de l'ancienne solidarité et une haine de l'ennemi commun qui les empêchaient d'aller aux extrémités auxquelles se livraient sans retenue les droit commun.

A Gandersheim, nos responsables étaient nos ennemis.

L'appareil administratif étant donc l'instrument, encore aiguisé, de l'oppression SS, la lutte collective était vouée à l'échec. (*EH*, 10)

'Ainsi', writes Antelme later in his testimony, 'ce qui était possible dans les camps où l'appareil était tenu par les détenus politiques ne devait pas l'être ici.' In Gandersheim, 'l'oppression et la misère étaient telles que la solidarité entre tous les politiques se trouvait elle-même compromise'. Entirely consumed by their physical labour, the men are unable to resist collectively, since 'pour organiser, pour penser, il faut encore avoir de la force et du temps'. 'La conscience de classe, l'esprit de solidarité sont encore l'expression d'une certaine santé qui reste aux opprimés. En dépit de quelques réveils, la conscience des détenus politiques avait bien des chances de devenir ici une conscience solitaire' (pp. 134–6).

Typically, Antelme's thinking does not stop here. Having established this initial opposition, he works through its dialectical consequence. If solidarity is impossible, and there is only individual survival, then individual survival itself is thought as affirming a kind of solidarity:

En face de cette coalition toute-puissante [i.e. the SS and the Kapos], notre objectif devenait le plus humble. C'était seulement de survivre. Notre combat, les meilleurs d'entre nous n'ont pu le mener que de façon individuelle. La solidarité même était devenue affaire individuelle. (p. 11)

The extremity of their situation means that the prisoners can resist, if at all, only as individuals; even in this fragmented resistance, however, they affirm a kind of ultimate, ontological solidarity, grounded in the absolute value of survival: 'Mais quoique solitaire, la résistance de cette conscience se poursuivait. Privé du corps des autres, privé progressivement du sien, chacun avait encore de la vie à défendre et à vouloir' (p. 136). The prisoner's agency is residual, minimal: in the 'almost biological' struggle for life, his will both is and is not active, as a common humanity affirms itself in the survival which both is and is not his. Just as the human must be thought as an irreducible and radically inclusive core of vulnerability, so must solidarity be re-conceptualized, in Antelme's dialectic, as precisely that which is declared in the poorest, most solitary struggle.

In this analysis, Antelme is positioning the prisoner or the deportee as a kind of ontological proletarian, and arguing that his solitary struggle already participates (with the immediate historicity he insistently attaches to the most intimate experience) in a resistance which refuses the logic of those who have reduced him to this state. Despised by his oppressor, who attempts to represent this oppression as the justified result of the prisoner's corruption, affirming in his struggle to survive the humanity from which this oppressor seeks to exclude him, the prisoner is, for Antelme, a principle of dignity precisely where dignity might be thought most utterly to have been lost. 'L'expérience de celui qui mange les épluchures' is thus defined by Antelme as 'une des situations ultimes de résistance', 'l'extrême expérience de la condition du prolétaire' (p. 101). To despise the prisoner who eats vegetable peelings because he has fallen from an essentially human self-respect is, says Antelme, to mistake the historical truth of the situation, which is that the destitute individual affirms in his destitution the struggle to liberate not just himself, but humanity as a whole from the logic of those who seek to divide it up by imposing this misery. This individual may experience this state as one of 'déchéance':

Mais on ne pouvait pas déchoir en ramassant des épluchures, pas plus que ne peut déchoir le prolétaire, 'matérialiste sordide', qui s'acharne à revendiquer, ne cesse de se battre, pour aboutir à sa libération et à celle de tous. Les perspectives de la libération de l'humanité dans son ensemble passent par ici, par cette 'déchéance'. (p. 101)

Destitution as a kind of residual solidarity, then: 'L'erreur de conscience n'est pas de déchoir, mais de perdre de vue que la déchéance doit être de tous et pour tous' (p. 102).[2]

While Antelme persists with notions of consciousness and struggle which seem to perpetuate an idea of solidarity more in tune with the active, fraternal version he presents as impossible, we need to see these notions in the context of his overall model. At times, the defiance of the prisoners clearly invokes their will, their remaining agency. The former medical student Jacques, for example, is celebrated for his refusal to compromise his integrity as a 'politique' in the face of the deprivations to which he is subjected, and is described as 'l'homme le plus achevé, le plus sûr de ses pouvoirs, des ressources de sa conscience et de la portée de ses actes, le plus fort' (p. 94). Antelme does not qualify this proud refusal, but we do need to nuance its apparent heroism. Its subject is a 'déchet', 'cet homme pourri, jaunâtre' (p. 94); his heroism is not separable from this destitution. Sure of his acts: but to act, here, is also (as Kofman reminds us) to piss, to shit, to achieve a freedom beyond the SS partly because of its attenuated, minimal connnection to the prisoners' will. 'Le SS s'incline devant l'indépendance apparente, la libre disposition de soi de l'homme qui pisse [...]; le SS ne sait pas qu'en pissant on s'évade' (p. 40), writes Antelme.

Kofman comments: 'Si Antelme multiplie ce genre de connotations, ce n'est pas qu'il s'y complaise de façon malsaine: c'est parce que "pisser" et "chier" étaient une manière de triompher des bourreaux qui ne pouvaient empêcher l'accomplissement de ces *actes* pas plus que de mourir'.[3] Before a certain degree of exhaustion is reached, the rhythms of the failing body can still just about be assumed by the prisoner as a contradictory act of defiance. But this does not assert a power denied those who have passed beyond this point: for this minimal agency is, in its poverty, inseparable from its own collapse. Accordingly, Jacques's defiance cannot be separated from the misery of those in whose name he resists, of whose number he also is. This is why, for example (again as Kofman points out), to act ethically in Antelme's account most often means to supplement the exhausted strength of a neighbour with what little remains of one's own: the solidarity so declared is meaningful precisely because this boundary is porous.[4]

There is indeed a kind of agency at work here, and it is valorized by Antelme; how could it not be? And why should we expect otherwise? To refuse exclusive, active heroism cannot mean the simple valorization of weakness *per se*: for this has no ethical or political potential at all. Rather, it is necessary to think as Antelme does, to correlate strength and weakness dialectically: to pick up moments of strength within surpassing weakness and, at the same time, to understand the strength of weakness as an ungraspable resistance to its own imposition, which in turn needs to be welcomed and nurtured by a further moment of strength (Blanchot's just 'Moi-Sujet'), and so on. Confronting an imaginary SS with the spectacle of Jacques's resistance, Antelme declares: 'Vous avez refait l'unité de l'homme. Vous avez fabriqué la conscience irréductible' (*EH*, 94–5). There is strength here, and unity and consciousness. And they are the eroded solidarity of the ontological proletariat, asserting a positive struggle as scraps of agency scattered among a wider resistance, itself carried on at an ontological level which is and is not theirs.

Antelme's Marxism, like his dialectic, thus takes a very particular form. While the Marxist-humanist emphasis on the construction of man as universal value is there, it is important to remember just how Antelme configures man: as residue, irreducible fragility, exposure. And so the solidarity affirmed in these declarations cannot simply be integrated into the confident solidarity-as-project which could found a community of resistance in a shared positive identity. Just as

Antelme's humanism finds its strength in its irreducible residuality, so is his model of solidarity grounded only in an erosion which it refuses to transcend. The affirmation of its force, then, affirms the force of the destitute in their very destitution; the victory of the deportee is an uncertain ontological victory which not only cannot be guaranteed, but is irreducible to thoughts of activity, achievement, project.[5]

On his return and his recovery, Antelme, like many, nevertheless responded to what he had experienced by joining the Parti Communiste Français. His membership would not last for long; the pain of his exclusion would last the rest of his life. The reasons for this exclusion are obscure, and certainly overdetermined. But it seems plausible that they had something to do with this unconventional, dislocated model of solidarity that Antelme derived as a necessity from his experience of the concentration camps. By way of an introduction to the subsequent political history of this model, I would now like briefly to sketch out the story of this exclusion, itself very much a story of eroded solidarity.

Duras had been a Party member since the autumn of 1944. 'Malgré cet exemple', writes Mascolo, 'et toutes les pressions amicales, Robert et moi tarderons à la suivre dans la voie de l'adhésion.' Having read only a little Marx, and sceptical of the PCF's Stalinism, they nonetheless hoped, in a term suggested at this time by Bataille, 'qu'un communisme *libéral* était possible'. A response to the revelation of the indivisibility of humanity, this communism, as Mascolo presents it, was anything but a dogma: 'Amalgame encore incertain de doutes et d'attentes, d'exigences et de refus non réductibles en concepts, et pas même en espoirs, on ne peut assigner à l'idée communiste naissante ce terme qui ferait d'elle un projet positif.' Nevertheless, 'selon une illusion très générale en ces années, nous pensions cependant que la victoire commune sur le nazisme [...] devait favoriser un retour à l'authenticité du mouvement révolutionnaire international'. And so:

Au printemps de 1946, à la fin de mars, nous résignant à ne pas nous préserver plus longtemps, Robert et moi, toute misère bien en vue, dans l'une de ces tristesses qui conviennent aux noces aussi bien qu'aux obsèques, marcherons vers la Place Saint-Sulpice (c'est un film), nous tenant par le bras — toujours ce rapport où chacun reprend force de l'appui qu'il offre à la faiblesse de l'autre — et franchirons le pas.[6]

With hindsight, Mascolo can anticipate the incompatibility that would become apparent between this radically open communism, impossibly grounded in the irreducible exposure of the human, and the increasingly hard-line Stalinism of the Party they had just joined. The eventual expulsion of Antelme, Mascolo and Duras, along with Monique Régnier (later to become Monique Antelme) and Bernard Guillochon, would result from a number of intertwined factors, some of which now seem substantively important, some unpleasantly intimate. But the most significant for our purposes is closely bound to the context of the concentration camps.[7]

The division in question first became apparent in the refusal of, notably, Antelme, Mascolo and Edgar Morin to accept the Party's Zhdanovite denunciation of the bourgeois decadence and complicity of all specifically intellectual and literary culture. But this position, inspired in part by Elio Vittorini, and set out in a 'Rapport au cercle des critiques' presented by Antelme in May 1948, was not, contrary to a frequent assumption, responsible for the subsequent exclusions.[8] Matters were, however, considerably worsened by a high-spirited evening in the café Bonaparte, in which fun was had at the expense of the Party hierarchy (in the person of Laurent Casanova), and which was reported to local sectional leaders, apparently by Semprun.[9] But the largest substantive factor in Antelme's expulsion relates directly to his concentrationary experiences.

On 12 November 1949, Rousset published in the *Figaro littéraire* a text entitled 'Au secours des déportés dans les camps soviétiques: un appel aux anciens déportés des camps nazis', in which he called especially upon those former prisoners who had testified publicly to their experience of the Nazi camps to join a commission of inquiry (to be composed exclusively of former political prisoners, of all persuasions) into the question of the existence of concentration camps in the Soviet Union.[10] Just as at the end of *L'Univers concentrationnaire*, Rousset names Antelme as one of those to whom his appeal is addressed. The vehemence with which the PCF responded to this text may be judged from the reply published by Pierre Daix in *Les Lettres françaises*, entitled 'Pierre Daix, matricule 59.807 à Mauthausen répond à David Rousset', following which Rousset sued *Les Lettres françaises* for libel.[11] For Antelme, then, the situation was delicate. Rousset was a friend, whom he even credited with introducing him to Marxism shortly before their respective deportations. But the call was not one to which he could easily respond from within the PCF.[12]

Antelme's reply was also published in the *Figaro littéraire*, on 19 November, under the title 'J'accepte sous conditions'. Contrary to the

Party line, Antelme does not rule out the existence of Soviet camps; he accepts Rousset's proposal, but subject to a number of conditions and remarks, including criticism of Rousset's publication of his appeal in the *Figaro littéraire*, where it 'ne peut pas ne pas constituer avant tout une manifestation d'anticommunisme'.[13] But these conditions (which, Antelme would later argue, took their cue from Soviet Foreign Minister Vishinsky, and which include the extension of Rousset's proposed inquiry to cover 'l'étude des divers régimes pénitentiaires et camps existant dans le monde, et surtout les conditions, le caractère du travail en régime capitaliste, dans les métropoles et dans leurs colonies' ('J'accepte', p. 189)) were not only not acceptable to Rousset: they were, conversely, insufficient for the PCF. Although he had cleared the article in advance with Pierre Daix (who in his response to Rousset had himself protested against the UN's refusal to accept the Soviet proposal of a commission of inquiry to investigate global labour conditions), Antelme's reply would seriously harm his reputation among his comrades.

In March 1950, Antelme found himself having to respond to the proposal, supported by 12 votes to 4 (with 5 abstentions) at an 'assemblée générale' of cell 722 (Saint-Germain-des-Prés), that he be expelled from the Party. He did so in a 'Mémoire justificatif', addressed to Raymond Guyot as secretary of the 'Fédération de la Seine du Parti communiste français'. From this text, it is possible to judge the anger felt by Antelme at his proposed exclusion; it is also clear that Antelme's relation to Rousset, to Semprun and to their collective status as former deportees was indeed crucial in his exclusion.[14]

In his defence, Antelme addresses various charges made against him as a result of his response to Rousset's campaign. He makes it abundantly clear that the reply published in the *Figaro littéraire*, and subsequently clarified by a letter to the *Lettres françaises*, had met with the support of such significant local Party figures as Pierre Daix and Jacques Martinet. Nevertheless, although his apparent association with the *Figaro littéraire* and with Rousset has tarnished his reputation in the eyes of some, Antelme has no regrets over his friendship: in part because, as mentioned above, 'c'est Rousset qui, le premier, exerça sur ma gangue bourgeoise le lent travail d'érosion de l'explication marxiste dont le camp devait me donner brutalement l'aveuglante confirmation' ('Mémoire justificatif', 237). But he distances himself quite explicitly from the Trotskyite position Rousset had previously held; states that he had attempted to attract Rousset to the PCF in 1946, when he was no longer a Trotskyite; and confirms that discussions around this time, together with Rousset's recent campaign on the Soviet camps, have led him to consider their friendship broken (p. 238).

It is clear throughout Antelme's text that he is struggling to reconcile what he sees as the human demands of friendship, and a more open understanding of solidarity, with the narrow positions of the Party. And, given that this open understanding was partly elaborated as a response to his experience of the concentration camps, it is horribly ironic that he should also have found himself charged (again, apparently, by Semprun) with criticizing the practices of the communist resistance in Buchenwald. Asked by the publisher José Corti to justify the policy implemented by the Buchenwald communists of selecting principally non-communists for the transports to the work camps, Antelme had presented a thorough, faithful defence. Corti's son, who had died at Dora, was a victim of this policy: his father's question was thus born of extreme pain. Subsequently, in conversation with Semprun, Antelme expressed the pain caused to him by Corti's grief, a mark of 'combien les nécessités du combat étaient parfois difficiles à assumer' (p. 244). Not to recognize that a distinction such as that at stake here between communists and non-communists is valid only as a terrible necessity, he argues, is to claim membership of 'une essence supérieure' (p. 245); it is not hard to appreciate the utter unacceptability of such a position to Antelme. But Semprun, apparently, expressed to other comrades his own shock at Antelme's sadness, which was subsequently transformed, says Antelme, into 'ce que dans son rapport ce malheureux appelle des attaques contre des camarades à Buchenwald' (p. 245).

Antelme's arguments seem to have had some effect, but did not prevail. Guyot's verdict, after an appeal by Daix, was one year's expulsion for Duras, Mascolo (who had both already left the Party), Régnier and Guillochon; for Antelme, 'blâme'. But by then it was too late. Invited to rejoin the Party in April 1951, Antelme and Régnier (by now parents to a new-born son) refused. As the disagreement over the role of communists in Buchenwald shows, the Party had proved unable to accommodate the enlarged sense of solidarity with human suffering which formed part of the lesson Antelme brought back from the camps. At stake, then, are two fundamentally opposed conceptions of communism.

The communism of the Party demanded, in effect, the annihilation of the politics of radical inclusivity that had brought Antelme, Mascolo and others to the Party in the first place. As Claude Roy phrased their dilemma: 'est-ce que nous pouvons rester communistes sans détruire en nous ce qui nous avait fait devenir communistes?'[15]. In Mascolo's words, 'Notre effort pour nous insérer dans la communauté éparse de ceux qui se réclament de l'idée communiste [...] aura donc duré peu de temps'.[16] But the difference is exactly this: the communism of Mascolo, Duras and Antelme demanded a 'communauté éparse' which the PCF could not provide. A communism grounded impossibly in the weakness of the suffering other, radically open, with no determinate end other than the specific, political contestation of the injustices by which this suffering is perpetuated, this communism is also a practice of the eroded solidarity derived by Antelme from his experience in Gandersheim. 'Sans qu'il en fût sans doute lui-même pleinement averti', writes Mascolo, 'Robert continuait d'être notre secret conseil, notre inspirateur. Rien de ce que nous aurions pu dire, écrire, ou entreprendre n'aurait pu être en contradiction avec le sens qu'il avait donné à ce qu'il avait vécu.'[17] And nowhere is this more true than in this attempt to practise an open form of community as a political and ethical response to the implication of Antelme's model of solidarity. If the radically destitute are excluded from any positive determination of solidarity, then another determination must be found, from which they are not excluded. This determination proved incompatible with the programme of the party supposedly fighting for the general liberation of humankind. But its political future was far from exhausted.

Untimely Communities

It is impossible, in the light of Antelme's interlinking of questions of solidarity and solitude, not to think of Camus; *La Peste*, Camus's own literary response to the experience of Occupation and Resistance, in which these questions are most extensively dramatized, was, like *L'Espèce humaine*, published in 1947. We might note, further, that the German civilian who extends his hand to Antelme and Jacques, has this gesture described in terms of a solitude which immediately discloses a historical revolt:

Et ce geste secret, solitaire, n'avait cependant pas un caractère privé, par opposition à l'action publique, immédiatement historique des SS. Tout rapport humain, d'un Allemand à l'un de nous, était le signe même d'une révolte décidée contre tout l'ordre SS. (*EH*, 80)

The connection is more than simply terminological: it is also biographical. The news of Antelme's arrest prompted Mascolo to find a safe place to hide the archives of the Mouvement national des prisonniers de guerre et déportés (MNPGD), helped immediately by Camus, who apparently stood watch while they were rescued from Antelme's apartment on the rue Saint-Benoît; Camus was also involved in the 1957 republication (instigated by Michel Gallimard) of *L'Espèce humaine*.[18] But the connection is more than simply biographical: it is also conceptual. As seen in Chapter 1 above, Camus, too, in his wartime *Lettres à un ami allemand*, insists on the necessity of some sort of solidarity as part of a refusal of the logic of the Nazi occupiers, in the name of a residual, resisting humanity. What is more, the solidarity which Camus advocates in response to the injustices of both the absurd universe and human cruelty can never itself cohere, is always riven by the solitude which calls it forth, the void of the absurd which it can never fill: as *La Peste* rather melodramatically makes clear, the struggle of revolt will be perpetual.

The comparison with Camus serves principally, however, to suggest just what it is that carries Antelme beyond his immediate post-1945 context, and makes him a key thinker for the turn of the twenty-first century. For, as we have noted, by the time of *L'Homme révolté*, Camus recuperates his residual, resisting humanity into a kind of solid permanence, tames the violence of just revolt with the explicitly trans-historical name of 'human nature' and fills out the inevitable fractures of rebellious solidarity with the metaphysical substance of fraternal resemblance. Antelme will never quite make this move. The weakness by which his model of the residual, resisting human is defined keeps this model from filling out the spaces of impossibly shared exposure which structure its articulated community. And, in this context, it is precisely this spacing that connects Antelme to the evolution of a thought and practice of radically open community in post-1945 French thought, just as it is the closure of these spaces by fusional resemblance that has distanced Camus from this very evolution. Antelme, then, while deeply engaged in this immediate post-war context, has found his thought in this area, as in the others explored in this study, also in harmony with intellectual and cultural developments around and since the time of his death in 1990. In this case, his thinking of solidarity as fractured, founded on the impossible basis of shared vulnerability, places him in a lineage which will lead to Nancy's work on community and Derrida's conception of contemporary political organization (with

Blanchot as the main connection in both cases); the details of his post-war political itinerary, moreover, reveal a practice of community which overlaps with and stimulates these theorizations. In this section, accordingly, I will first outline this itinerary, before describing the major theorizations of community with which it is entwined; subsequently, I will look in some detail at texts by Nancy and Derrida in which Antelme's influence may be discerned.

Following his expulsion from the PCF, Antelme's political activities (as well as those of his close friends) remain determined by the motor of this painful exclusion, namely their other, non-totalitarian understanding of communism, not so much a positive doctrine as a ceaseless opening or exposure, itself the necessary consequence of the revelation of the irreducible unity of 'l'espèce humaine'. As we have seen, Mascolo gives Antelme as the emblem of this other understanding of communism, which, inaugurated as political practice in this moment of exclusion, comes to dominate the political interventions—and the practice of community—of this *groupuscule* for the next forty years.

The first event which prompts the elaboration of this other, open version of community is the war in Algeria. In 1955 Antelme was one of the co-founders of the 'Comité d'action contre la poursuite de la guerre en Afrique du Nord'; in 1958 he participated in the protests against the return to power of De Gaulle on the basis of the unrest in Algeria. Antelme's piece 'Les principes à l'épreuve', published at this time in the first number of *Le 14 Juillet*, is a striking condensation of the key elements of the politics he and his friends pursued in this post-war period. Showing his Hegelian influences, but in an idiom which strangely resembles that of Levinas (and so again indicates Antelme's extraordinary anticipation of later intellectual trends), he insists that 'On n'oublie pas que l'histoire de chacun se fait à travers le besoin d'être reconnu sans limite; l'amitié désigne cette capacité infinie de reconnaissance [...]. Reconnaître autrui est le souverain bien, et non un pis-aller' (*TI*, 34). His opposition to the doctrinaire position of the PCF (anticipating debates around May 1968) is visceral ('Le Parti communiste inspire l'horreur' (p. 37)); his support for 'cette guerre menée par des prolétaires exsangues', the comrades of Jacques, unequivocal (p. 36); and the vision of an other communism (an 'idea', as for Mascolo, and, interestingly, residual) resounding: 'Le communisme est aujourd'hui étouffé, défiguré, ensanglanté dans le crime. L'idée reste. Les forces de la république universelle, latentes, immobiles, sont là. Le besoin de cette république s'affirmera' (p. 38). This 'république universelle' is a radical demand, incompatible with the eschato-logically prescribed *terminus ad quem* of the Party line; it is the open, articulated community of 'prolétaires exsangues' first elaborated in *L'Espèce humaine*.

It is also, moreover, the driving force behind this particular political trajectory. After opposition to De Gaulle, Antelme signed the 'Déclaration sur le droit à l'insoumission dans la guerre d'Algérie' (the 'Manifeste des 121') in 1960, and a subsequent collective 'Lettre au juge d'instruction' insisting that all the signatories of the 'Manifeste' be treated equally (i.e., as equally responsible) before the law.[19] Developing the central theses of this document, he composed in 1967 an 'Appel international pour une rupture', in opposition to the war in Vietnam. Entitled 'En vue de la défaite américaine', this supports the fight of the Vietnamese people by affirming once more 'le droit à l'insoumission' on the part initially of Americans refusing to fight in Vietnam, before, as in 1958, linking the key terms of friendship and openness, and anticipating the ethical idiom of the philosophical generation in the process of establishing itself (Derrida was, incidentally, one of the signatories of this text): 'Droit de refuser, devoir d'aider qui refuse: à ces hommes le respect est dû, et l'aide de tous, et l'amitié. Les frontières seront ouvertes. C'est la loi qui est au-dessus de toute loi. Elle est déjà notre règle.'[20]

Antelme's subsequent political interventions comprise, essentially, his involvement in the events of May 1968, as a member of the 'Comité d'action étudiants-écrivains' formed in the Sorbonne (the significance of the May events for the theorization of open community will be discussed below); and a text read before the 'tribunal permanent des forces armées de Bordeaux-Aquitaine' in June 1974, in support of Bernard Rémy, a former 'professeur de lettres' at a national service air base, who had founded a 'groupe d'informations sur l'armée', had deserted in 1972, and had been sentenced to eighteen months in prison.[21] Here, Antelme deploys a human rights rhetoric which is re-oriented importantly in the direction of his residual humanism, such that the 'man' who is the subject of these rights is, characteristically, an unnamed, unidentifiable, but irreducible residue: 'avant son nom, son apparence, etc., avant d'être nommé, il est, nous le reconnaissons en nous-mêmes, comme un sujet de droits' (*TI*, 40). Antelme's support for Rémy in this text takes the form of a critique of technological capitalism, and the evocation, once again, of a radically open community: 'Personne n'est exclu de la société qu'évoquent les idées de Bernard Rémy, elle est ouverte, chacun y reconnaît l'autre, ils travaillent ensemble, ils s'aident, se saluent, se connaissent, se savent: je sais que l'autre existe là-bas, il est mon frère' (p. 42). This piece displays a number of characteristics which allow us to summarize the recurrent elements of Antelme's principal post-war political interventions. In it, Antelme mobilizes the key notion of unconditional recognition of the other, uses friendship as the name of this recognition, and articulates a model of solidarity or fraternity which is defined not by resemblance but by openness. And it is precisely in such terms that others around Antelme in this political journey will indeed approach the question of community.

For this journey is not just Antelme's: it is also that of Duras, Mascolo, Blanchot (from 1958) and others. The theorizations of community as radically open, grounded impossibly in weakness rather than a proud collective project, come mostly from Mascolo and, especially, Blanchot; in the 1980s, Blanchot provides the helpful terms 'la communauté négative' and, citing Bataille (on whom much of this thinking draws), 'la communauté de ceux qui n'ont pas de communauté' to name this notion of community as shared dislocation.[22] But the first of these theorizations appears just after the republication of L'Espèce humaine: in the opposition to De Gaulle's prise de pouvoir in 1958.

In the first number of Le 14 Juillet (alongside Antelme's 'Les principes à l'épreuve'), Mascolo makes an important connection: between refusal as political position, and the fractured collectivity which results from this position. Perhaps developing a rhetoric employed by Antelme in 1945, when he had opposed violent retributions against German prisoners of war with a vehement 'non', Mascolo demands: 'Que notre parole d'abord, notre plus forte et plus faible, notre plus lucide et plus naïve, notre plus volontaire et plus injustifiable, que notre premier et dernier mot soit NON'.[23] The most significant elaboration of the shattered community of refusal comes, however, in the second number of Le 14 Juillet, in the form of Blanchot's 'Le refus'.

For Blanchot (in a move which will later become extremely familiar, not only in Blanchot's thinking, but in Derrida's too), the 'NON' for which Mascolo had called is an affirmation: it affirms in the first place the articulated shape of this collectivity, whose refusal constitutes an irreducible but ungraspable bond which unites precisely by its failure to do so:

Les hommes qui refusent et qui sont liés par la force du refus, savent qu'ils ne sont pas encore ensemble. Le temps de l'affirmation commune leur a précisément été enlevé. Ce qui leur reste, c'est l'irréductible refus, l'amitié de ce Non certain, inébranlable, rigoureux, qui les tient unis et solidaires.[24]

The echoes of Antelme here are considerable: not only of *L'Espèce humaine*, in the irreducible bond which cannot constitute itself as such, or the absence of the time in which a communal project of solidarity might be founded (which will be discussed in detail below), but also, in this rhetoric of 'amitié' as the name for this articulated relationship (the importance of which to Blanchot's thinking is of course immense), of 'Les principes à l'épreuve', as discussed above. Indeed, Bident states categorically that Blanchot's argument here is influenced by Antelme, and specifically by this text: 'Dégager le refus de tout nihilisme, c'est sous la condition de Robert Antelme, de l'esprit de *L'Espèce humaine* et plus explicitement du texte publié par lui dans le premier numéro [of *Le 14 Juillet*] que Blanchot va le faire'.[25] Accordingly, Blanchot's refusal grounds itself, along the lines of Antelme's eroded solidarity, in a weakness which is not appropriable as a foundation:

Quand nous refusons, nous refusons par un mouvement sans mépris, sans exaltation, et anonyme, autant qu'il se peut, car le pouvoir de refuser ne s'accomplit pas à partir de nous-mêmes, ni en notre seul nom, mais à partir d'un commencement très pauvre qui appartient d'abord à ceux qui ne peuvent pas parler.[26]

The gesture of refusal thus takes place on the ungraspable basis of what Antelme terms in 1967 'la loi qui est au-dessus de toute loi' ('En vue de la défaite américaine', 100); the community so founded remains marked by its necessary absence, riven by the separation which is also the condition of its poor solidarity.

Ten years later, many of those who had come together around *Le 14 Juillet*, and had subsequently militated in support of the Algerian fight for independence, found themselves together once more, in the Comité d'action étudiants-écrivains (CAEE) formed in the Sorbonne in May 1968. The May events as a whole, of course, present an image of just the kind of fractured, open community whose history is here in question; it might even be argued that it was precisely this inchoate, even acephalic quality that allowed the protestors something of their force.

Consequently, key texts published in the CAEE's journal *Comité* (and subsequently attributed to Blanchot) mobilize the recurrent themes of this fractured solidarity. In 'En état de guerre', for example, we find again the weakness, fragility, and dispersal of the 'Nous' of radical refusal: 'Aux autres, c'est-à-dire, si possible, à nous, la pénurie, le défaut de parole, la puissance de rien'. In 'Affirmer la rupture', refusal affirms the articulated, spaced quality of this (non-)community, being 'un refus qui affirme [...], une affirmation qui ne s'arrange pas, mais qui dérange et se dérange, ayant rapport avec le désarrangement ou le désarroi ou encore le non-structurable'. The rupture thus affirmed is, as another title has it, a 'Rupture du temps', a mystical-cum-Leninist view of revolution as 'arrêt, suspens', recalling the temporal impossibility which marks both Blanchot's 1958 elaboration of 'Le refus', and Antelme's erosion of solidarity. Finally, the communism affirmed in this revolution is a 'communisme sans héritage', defined in opposition to the PCF as 'ce qui exclut (et s'exclut de) toute communauté déjà constituée', not least 'la classe prolétarienne, communauté sans autre dénominateur commun que la pénurie, l'insatisfaction, le manque en tous sens'.[27]

These theorizations by Mascolo and Blanchot elaborate around Antelme's political itinerary a notion of negative, articulated, or spaced community which thus not only accompanies his own activism, but at the very least echoes, and arguably indeed responds to, his own interventions both in *L'Espèce humaine* and elsewhere. It seems clear, therefore, that the model of fractured solidarity disclosed throughout Antelme's testimony at least gives onto the shape of the communities of refusal theorized by Blanchot and Mascolo in 1958 and 1968. But the proximity of Antelme to these theorizations, his own contemporary use of their idioms, and the influence he exerted on the group during this period, all suggest that the connection might reasonably be thought as more than one of anticipation. What I would now like to argue is that, beyond his own political trajectory, a similar relationship of uncanny anticipation, and even arguably influence, may hold between Antelme's model of solidarity and work by major later thinkers to whom he displays less close biographical but, I shall try to show, significant intellectual connections. The links I will be tracing are delicate; they are woven into the filigree of intellectual transmission. It is not a matter of a direct or obvious legacy. But, if we accept that such transmission may at times be fragile or indirect, then the links are there to be traced.

The first of the recent thinkers I propose to consider in these terms is Jean-Luc Nancy. The connections between Blanchot and Nancy around the question of community form a tight, if at times ambiguous weave: Nancy's 1983 essay *La Communauté désœuvrée*, which draws principally on Bataille, cites Blanchot's 1968 definition of 'le communisme sans héritage', as quoted above; Blanchot's *La Communauté inavouable*, published towards the end of 1983, takes Nancy's essay as its explicit starting point; Nancy's use of the term 'désœuvrée' is derived from Blanchot, and so on.[28] And given the links between Blanchot and Antelme on this question around and before 1968, there is certainly a connection (albeit appropriately spaced) between Nancy and Antelme here. More substantively, Nancy cites Antelme as perhaps the 'meilleur témoin' of his central argument: namely that death, in its ungraspability, forms a limit to fusion and immanence and, as such, determines the very possibility of community as resistant to positive thematization.[29] Accordingly, Nancy's approach, in which community is defined precisely as the articulation of its 'members' by the mortal exposure they impossibly share, offers intriguing resemblances and points of contact to Antelme's riven community as we have traced it here.

The type of community which Nancy wishes to reject, which he generally terms 'fusional', 'totalitarian' or 'immanent', is in a sense the fraternal model of solidarity which is rendered untenable for Antelme by his experience of Gandersheim: community as common project, as the *œuvre* of man in which his essence could be realized, and which Nancy initially associates with all formally constituted oppositional movements laying claim to the name of 'communism'.[30] In its slippage away from any positive ontological foundation, community for Nancy 'is' the loss of communion in the unworkable exposure to the death of *autrui*. As his approving reference to Antelme as perhaps the 'meilleur témoin' to this argument implies, Nancy's community has specific features in common with Antelme's eroded solidarity: both are (un)founded in impossibly shared exposure, unthinkable as project and resistant to the exclusionary, murderous logic of positive identity. Equally, the shape of this thought of community displays the paradoxical coincidence of separation and connection which runs from Antelme's eroded solidarity through the theory and pratice of community in his subsequent politics—namely, it is articulated, spaced, connection in separation. Talking of 'singularities' to emphasize that the 'members' of this 'community' are not thinkable as 'subjects' (lacking the grounding substance implied by this notion), Nancy anticipates his later work with Jean-Christophe Bailly on 'la comparution', and defines this community in the following terms: 'La communauté est la présentation du détachement (ou du retranchement), de la distinction qui n'est pas l'individuation, mais la finitude comparaissant'.[31] An articulated grouping determined by 'la finitude comparaissant': eroded solidarity.

The transmission of this structure, from *L'Espèce humaine*, *via* Antelme's later political interventions and the theorizations of community especially by Blanchot which accompany these interventions, to this recent thinking of community as other than grounded in positively shared identity, gives us something of the actuality of Antelme. If the links between Antelme and Nancy run largely through Blanchot, it is also, and therefore, the case that, as he acknowledges, Nancy's attempt to think a non-fusional community founded impossibly in exposure to mortality ultimately owes much to the eroded solidarity Antelme elaborates in *L'Espèce humaine*. For confirmation of this, we might turn to another uncanny anticipation. Four or five years after his return from Dachau, Antelme wrote to Mascolo in terms which it is worth citing at length. For here, in a letter from 1949–50, we may already find astonishing resonances with the later thought of Blanchot (on friendship, community, death and the neuter) and Nancy (as the spaced community introduced by the shared ungraspability of mortality). *Mutatis mutandis* (although the specific differences are not so great, and are due mostly to intellectual context), this letter would almost present Antelme as a ghostly forerunner of Levinas, Derrida, Blanchot, Nancy—were it not for the influence his thought has also exerted. Not just uncanny, then: also decisive, and certainly under-recognized.

Dionys, je voudrais te dire que je ne pense pas l'amitié comme une chose positive, je veux dire comme une valeur, mais bien plus, je veux dire comme un état, une identification, donc une multiplication de la mort, une multiplication de l'interrogation, le lieu miraculeusement le plus neutre d'où percevoir et sentir la constante d'inconnu, le lieu où la différence dans ce qu'elle a de plus aigu ne vit — comme on l'entendrait à la 'fin de l'histoire' —, ne s'épanouit qu'au cœur de son contraire — proximité de la mort.[32]

The topos of the ghost is indeed a tempting one here, talk of the afterlife or survival of Antelme's thought almost unavoidable; and so it is perhaps inevitable that this account of this survival should conclude with its resonance within a key elaboration of such figures as, precisely, political: Derrida's *Spectres de Marx*.

Appropriately in this context, the line from Antelme to Derrida is just as delicately woven as that from Antelme to Nancy. Derrida has recently mentioned *L'Espèce humaine* in an interview, describing it as 'un témoignage majeur'.[33] More significantly, Derrida was, as we have seen, one of the signatories to Antelme's 1967 'En vue de la défaite américaine'. And the thought of open community, in the name of a law beyond all law, which we saw above elaborated by Antelme in this tract, and which is derived from the thesis and political afterlife of *L'Espèce humaine*, is what we can find resonating—quite precisely, I will argue—a quarter of a century later, in *Spectres de Marx*.

To demonstrate this resonance, I propose to discuss a form of shared political action which Derrida describes in this text, and which, like Blanchot's 'hommes qui refusent', or Antelme's solidarity with those Americans refusing to fight in Vietnam, seeks to resist the violence of global capitalist imperialism: what Derrida calls the 'nouvelle Internationale'. For an initial echo, we might note Derrida's declaration that 'Ce qui s'appelle ici, sous le nom de nouvelle Internationale, c'est ce qui rappelle à l'amitié d'une alliance sans institution':[34] already in his letter to Mascolo of 1949–50, again in 'Les principes à l'épreuve' in 1958, and again in 1967, 'amitié' was Antelme's word for this disestablished opposition, in which 'les frontières seront ouvertes' ('En vue de la défaite américaine', 100). Following 'Les principes à l'épreuve', as we have seen, it would also become Blanchot's in 'Le refus' (subsequently, supplemented by its Bataillean significance, naming the 1971 collection in which this is republished). The Blanchot of the late 1950s is, as we will soon see, a considerable presence in *Spectres de Marx*; cumulatively, then, it is hard not to conclude that this 'amitié' (explored in detail in Derrida's next major work, *Politiques de l'amitié*) makes its way into Derrida's response to contemporary politics *via* the itinerary we have just been tracing.

In addition to the idea that political action might take place as a kind of radically open friendship, there is a more particular sense in which the figures of oppositional organization at work in *Spectres de Marx* may be related to Antelme's thought in this area. For, once we examine it in more detail, it becomes clear that Derrida's approach here displays intimate connections to those we have followed along Antelme's political and intellectual itinerary. Derrida defines the 'nouvelle Internationale' in the following terms:

C'est un lien d'affinité, de souffrance et d'espérance, un lien encore discret, presque secret, comme autour de 1848, mais de plus en plus visible — on en a plus d'un signe. C'est un lien intempestif et sans statut, sans titre et sans nom, à peine public s'il n'est pas clandestin, sans contrat, '*out of joint*', sans coordination, sans parti, sans patrie, sans communauté nationale (Internationale avant, à travers et au-delà de toute détermination nationale), sans co-citoyenneté, sans appartenance commune à une classe.[35]

Of most significance here are, first, the structure of this bond which is not one; secondly, the language of its articulation; and thirdly, its essential untimeliness.

In the first place, then, Derrida's 'new International', like Antelme's eroded solidarity, Blanchot's refusal and Nancy's community, offers another articulated structure, bonds of impoverishment and silence which are thinkable as connections only to the extent that they separate, deprive those whom they bind of anything which could secure this binding. Secondly, this spaced community is sketched in an idiom which, with its repeated use of the disjunctive 'sans', recalls Antelme by echoing Blanchot's 'les hommes qui refusent', itself, as seen above, elaborated in the light of *L'Espèce humaine* and 'Les principes à l'épreuve'. Derrida's 'sans contrat, "*out of joint*", sans coordination, sans parti, sans patrie, sans communauté nationale [...], sans co-citoyenneté, sans appartenance commune à une classe' echoes by exaggeration Blanchot's 'mouvement sans mépris, sans exaltation, et anonyme, autant qu'il se peut',[36] especially given both the similarity of the grouping being advocated and Derrida's avowed fascination for Blanchot's use of 'sans'.[37] When this grouping is first introduced, indeed, the link to Blanchot is trebled: in the disjunctive nature of the group, in the consequent repetition of 'sans' and in the treatment of the word 'communism'. Derrida writes: 'L'alliance d'un *rejoindre* sans conjoint, sans organisation, sans parti, sans nation, sans Etat, sans propriété (le "communisme" que nous surnommerons plus loin la nouvelle Internationale)'.[38] These scare quotes constitute a typographical reference to Blanchot's 1959 'La fin de la philosophie' (already mentioned by Derrida),[39] which, in its slightly modified 1971 reprint as 'Lentes funérailles', includes the following note: 'Communisme ici et nécessairement entre guillemets: on n'appartient pas au communisme, et le communisme ne se laisse pas désigner par ce qui le nomme'.[40] *Via* his articulated grouping, 'sans', and this 'communisme sans héritage', we travel from Derrida back to the Blanchot of 1958–9, then; which is to say, as we have seen, also to Antelme.

Most of all, however, it is Derrida's repeated insistence on the untimely nature of this 'new International' that allows a key, substantive link back to Blanchot and, from there, to Antelme. In a spectral gloss to Blanchot's 'Les trois paroles de Marx', for example (already quoted in Chapter 1), Derrida writes: 'Maintenir ensemble ce qui ne tient pas ensemble [...], cela ne peut se penser [...] que dans un temps du présent dis-loqué, à la jointure d'un temps radicalement dis-joint, sans conjonction assurée'.[41] This dislocated present moment without presence obsesses *Spectres de Marx*, in which it is refigured as the quasi-messianic boding forth of the just future. It is also, I would argue, traceable in part to Antelme. 'Maintenir ensemble ce qui ne tient pas ensemble': this is Antelme's eroded solidarity, and all that follows from it. For the refusal that Blanchot develops under the aegis of Antelme in the late 1950s is itself articulated by this empty present: we may recall that Blanchot's 'hommes qui refusent' know that they are not yet together, because, as he puts it, 'le temps de l'affirmation commune leur a précisément été enlevé'.[42] And what is it that makes the fraternal model of solidarity unavailable to Antelme and his comrades? The lack of strength—and, crucially, the lack of time: 'pour organiser, pour penser, il faut encore avoir de la force et du temps' (*EH*, 135). The time which is lacking is that fusional moment in which solidarity might cohere, in which camaraderie might found itself in and as a common substance and a shared project, which could take place right here, right now.[43] The only time available to Antelme and his comrades, and hence to Blanchot's 'hommes qui refusent', and hence to Derrida's new Internationalists, is an other time: that of destitution, of friendship as understood here first by Antelme—a time of vacancy, opening, exposure. The time of revolution, for Blanchot in 1968, inasmuch as revolution is a 'Rupture du temps'; the future to which Antelme calls in 1967, vowing to protect by any means necessary 'l'avenir là où il est menacé' ('En vue de la défaite américaine', 101). But not, crucially, the future of transcendence, not the inevitable eschatological victory of the slave—for these are just fantasies of the present deferred, the future (even unto death) brought in anticipation within the grasp of the existential subject. Rather, this always empty future, which is the time of accompaniment, is also the fractured now in which Jacques and his comrades triumph: a moment out of time, a present without presence, the non-time of erosion, of the destitute, whose force is necessarily untimely, unavailable in its irreducible vulnerability.[44]

The dislocated present of *Spectres de Marx*, this is the time of Antelme's eroded solidarity: the time in which his comrades suffer, but in which, and whereby, their resistance to the regime imposing this suffering is affirmed. And this is also, in another sense, Antelme's future. The lineage of these articulated or spaced communities is not, nor can it be, a matter simply of direct influence or inheritance—not least because such directness, unhindered fusional communication of a shared interiority, is precisely what they reject. Rather, I have tried here to draw out how the re-elaboration in *L'Espèce humaine* of fraternal solidarity as an open, riven community of exposure and friendship resonates in the world beyond the camps, partly by inspiring and verbalizing a particular strand of the history of the French left, and partly by feeding into subsequent philosophical considerations of related questions. In a sense, Antelme finds in these considerations a belated solidarity, which echoes with the approaches he elaborated within and around the political community (never formalized as such) of which he was a key part. It is inevitable, perhaps, that Antelme's thought should come to resonate now, posthumously: for it is, in part, a thought of connection as separation, of friendship as radically open contact in a way figured all too well by the pathos of this delay.

It is also, however, a thought which insists that we transfigure this 'now' which we might take to be ours: by understanding it, in turn, not as a moment of possession, but as an opening, a dispossession— the always futural emptiness which gives us the chance to respond, across the separation, to those whose destitution demands redress.

Notes to Chapter 2

1. Theodor W. Adorno, *Negative Dialectics* (1966), trans. E. B. Ashton (London: Routledge, 1996), 362.
2. This analysis is set out (and its Marxist and Hegelian infrastructure made especially clear) in Antelme's 1948 piece 'Pauvre — Prolétaire — Déporté': see *TI*, 25–32.
3. Kofman, *Paroles suffoquées*, 73.
4. Ibid. 61, as discussed in *Readings (I)* above.
5. In Rousset's *L'Univers concentrationnaire*, despite acknowledgement of the difficulties facing organized resistance within Buchenwald, the German communists in particular remain able to effect such resistance. It seems likely, therefore, given the prominence of *L'Univers concentrationnaire* at the time, that Rousset's account is the context Antelme had in mind when warning his readers what kind of solidarity they should not expect in his description of Gandersheim.
6. Mascolo, *Autour d'un effort de mémoire*, 71, 71, 65–6, 71, 73.
7. The full story of these expulsions is located in the PCF archives, in a file headed

'Affaire Duras-Mascolo-Antelme'. It is set out in detail in Gérard Streiff, *Procès stalinien à Saint-Germain-des-Prés* (Paris: Syllepse, 1999).

8. The 'Rapport' is reproduced in *Lignes, 33: Avec Dionys Mascolo* (Paris: Hazan, Mar. 1998), 25–39. Vittorini's defence of the relative independence of cultural production was set out in his 'Letter to Togliatti', published in his review *Il Politecnico* in Jan. 1947, and reaffirmed in 'Jean Gratien' (Dionys Mascolo) and Edgar Morin, 'Une interview d'Elio Vittorini' (*Les Lettres françaises*, 27 June 1947, 1, 7). Streiff (*Procès*, 26) and Pierre Daix (*Les Hérétiques du PCF* (Paris: Robert Laffont, 1980), 186) confirm the insistence of Laurent Casanova, then responsible for the role of intellectuals in the Party, that differences over the cultural question could not lead to political sanctions.

9. The evening is described in Streiff, *Procès*, 16. In response to press coverage of Adler's 1998 biography of Duras, Semprun defended his role in the affair in 'Non, je n'ai pas "dénoncé" Marguerite Duras', *Le Monde*, 26 June 1998, 16. Monique Antelme replied to Semprun's account in 'Jorge Semprun n'a pas dit la vérité', *Le Monde*, 8 July 1998, 11.

10. Rousset's text is reproduced in *Lignes* 2 (N.S.) (Paris: Léo Scheer, May 2000), 143–60.

11. Pierre Daix, 'Pierre Daix, matricule 59.807 à Mauthausen répond à David Rousset', *Les Lettres françaises*, 17 Nov. 1949, 1, 4.

12. Rousset was aware of this, as he explained in a letter to Antelme of 21 Nov.: 'Je ne pouvais pas ne pas te citer. Longtemps j'ai hésité. Je savais ce que cela signifierait pour toi. Mais l'affection que je te porte se fonde sur l'estime que j'ai de toi et il fallait donc que je te cite' (David Rousset, 'Lettre à Robert Antelme', *Lignes* 3 (N.S.) (Paris: Léo Scheer, Oct. 2000), 183–6 (186)).

13. Robert Antelme, 'J'accepte sous conditions', *Lignes* 3 (N.S.), 187–91 (188).

14. Robert Antelme, 'Mémoire justificatif au Parti Communiste Français au sujet de son exclusion', *Lignes 33: Avec Dionys Mascolo*, 229–49 (231).

15. Roy, *Nous*, 124.

16. Mascolo, *Autour d'un effort de mémoire*, 82.

17. Ibid. 79.

18. See ibid. 45; and Olivier Todd, *Albert Camus: une vie*, édition revue et corrigée (Paris: Gallimard, Folio, 1996), 477.

19. 'Déclaration sur le droit à l'insoumission dans la guerre d'Algérie', *Lignes* 33, 84–7; 'Lettre au juge d'instruction', ibid. 89–90.

20. 'En vue de la défaite américaine', ibid. 99–101 (100).

21. 'L'homme comme sujet des droits', *TI*, 39–43. Rémy published, notably, *L'Homme des casernes* (Paris: Maspero, 1975) and *Journal de prison: espacements* (Paris: Hachette, 1977).

22. 'La communauté négative' is the title of the first section of Blanchot's *La Communauté inavouable* (Paris: Minuit, 1983), 7–47; the phrase 'la communauté de ceux qui n'ont pas de communauté', attributed to 'G. B.', comes on p. 9. See also Alphonso Lingis, *The Community of Those Who Have Nothing in Common* (Bloomington, IN: Indiana University Press, 1994), whose version of community as impossibly shared exposure resonates importantly with Antelme's: 'The touch of consolation opens the path, in the time of endurance and suffering, to an accompaniment in dying and finds brotherhood with the other in the last limit of his or her destitution' (pp. 178–9).

23. Dionys Mascolo, 'Refus inconditionnel', in *A la recherche d'un communisme de pensée*, 147–9 (149). Compare Antelme's 'Vengeance?': 'Aussi, aux folies de la vengeance, aux abstentions secrètes, aux lâchetés des indemnes, nous disons: non' (*TI*, 24).

24. Maurice Blanchot, 'Le refus' (1958), in *L'Amitié*, 130–1 (130).

25. Bident, *Maurice Blanchot*, 381.

26. Blanchot, 'Le refus', 131.

27. These texts are collected in *Lignes* 33; the page references are, respectively: 'En état de guerre', 134–6 (136); 'Affirmer la rupture', 136–7 (137); 'Rupture du temps: révolution' (158); and 'Le Communisme sans héritage', 147–8 (148).

28. See, respectively, Jean-Luc Nancy, *La Communauté désœuvrée* (1986), nouvelle édition revue et augmentée (Paris: Christian Bourgois, 1999), 25; Blanchot, *La Communauté inavouable*, 9; Nancy, *La Communauté désœuvrée*, 78. On the relationship between Blanchot and Nancy here, see Hill, *Blanchot: Extreme Contemporary*, 198–204.

29. Nancy, *La Communauté désœvrée*, 88 n. 26.

30. Ibid. 14.

31. Ibid. 74–5. See also Jean-Christophe Bailly and Jean-Luc Nancy, *La Comparution* (Paris: Christian Bourgois, 1991).

32. Mascolo, *Autour d'un effort de mémoire*, 23–4.

33. 'Jacques Derrida: Le cinéma et ses fantômes', interview with Derrida by Antoine de Baecque and Thierry Jousse, in *Cahiers du cinéma* 556 (Apr. 2001), 75–85 (84).

34. Jacques Derrida, *Spectres de Marx*, 142.

35. Ibid. 141–2.

36. Blanchot, 'Le refus', 131.

37. See Jacques Derrida, 'Pas' (1976), in *Parages*, 19–116, esp. 90–2.

38. Derrida, *Spectres de Marx*, 58.

39. Ibid. 39.

40. Blanchot, *L'Amitié*, 101 n. 1.

41. Derrida, *Spectres de Marx*, 41–2.

42. Blanchot, 'Le refus', 130.

43. Discussing Blanchot's account of his first meeting with Antelme, Simon Critchley also makes the implicit link to Derrida: 'Friendship, unlike camaraderie, is bound up with an experience of time's passing, of time not as the explosion of the *Augenblick* or *Jetztpunkt*, or indeed the mystical *scintilla dei* so dear to the various fatal political romanticisms of this century [...] but, rather, time as the experience of passage, procrastination, temporisation, delay, one might even say *différance*' (Simon Critchley, *Ethics—Politics—Subjectivity: Essays on Derrida, Levinas and Contemporary French Thought* (London: Verso, 1999), 256–7).

44. This is also (to loop the loop) the time of friendship, for Derrida (as for Blanchot): see Derrida, *Politiques de l'amitié* (Paris: Galilée, 1994), 31. While Derrida links his thinking on friendship with those of Blanchot and Nancy on community, we should note his reservation about the inevitable persistence of the fraternal within any notion of community: see esp. 56 n. 1 and 330–1. For Derrida, friendship, rather than community, names this fractured solidarity.

Readings (II)

Perec

Sitting on a train in May 1970, Georges Perec sketched a plan for what would become *W ou le souvenir d'enfance*. After the title, a short line represents the first part of the work: '1: W pour Robert Antelme'. Enigmatic phrases suggest the content of the third; among these, 'absence de repères (cf. Antelme)'.[1] As Philippe Lejeune points out, this is a reference to Antelme's 'Avant-propos', in which the specific horror of Gandersheim is defined as 'obscurité, manque absolu de repère, solitude, oppression incessante, anéantissement lent'.[2] This 1970 reference to Antelme is not at all surprising: for seven years earlier, Perec had published 'Robert Antelme ou la vérité de la littérature', a piece which is preceded only by Blanchot's 'L'indestructible' in the history of major critical responses to *L'Espèce humaine*; a piece which, indeed, quotes this very extract.[3]

With extraordinary acuity, Perec offers in this piece what remains the most exact account of Antelme's reworking of the notion of solidarity, and defines succinctly the reasons which necessitate this move. As his title implies, he will go on to consider the significance of *L'Espèce humaine* for the writing of testimony, and indeed for literature in general; in order to do so, he needs first to establish the fractured commonality to which Antelme bears witness. After summarizing Antelme's description of the administrative regime of Gandersheim, he presents economically the impossibility of conventional solidarity: 'L'organisation politique, c'était la sauvegarde assurée d'un certain pourcentage de la population du camp. Le règne des droits communs, c'est l'impossibilité de toute organisation' (*TI*, 182). Perec is here drawing a contrast with Rousset's model, in which, as we have noted, some solidarity remains possible; such accounts, however, falsify 'le mécanisme concentrationnaire', according to Perec, since 'nous le voyons à travers des yeux privilégiés' (p. 182). Solidarity is not a given; and its fragmentation in Gandersheim gives rise to an unusually stark testimony:

La solidarité n'est pas une évidente métaphysique, ni un impératif catégorique.

Elle est liée à des conditions précises. Nécessaire à la survie du groupe, parce qu'elle en assure la cohésion, il suffit qu'elle soit interdite pour que l'univers concentrationnaire apparaisse dans sa logique la plus pure. (p. 182)

Still following Antelme, Perec goes on to describe the necessary transformation of solidarity from active communal project into passive, residual resistance. Tracing the powerlessness of the SS before Antelme's ineradicable humanity, he writes that 'cette revendication de l'espèce humaine, cette conscience première de l'impossible contestation de l'homme [...] appellent une solidarité nouvelle non plus active, puisque le rôle des kapos est de l'interdire, mais implicite: qui naît de ce que les déportés subissent *ensemble*' (p. 186). As for Antelme, then, this 'implicit' solidarity implies the eventual defeat of the SS: 'C'est dans cette unité, dans cette conscience, que le SS va se perdre. C'est ce qu'il ne peut comprendre: dans ce monde qui doit consacrer la déchéance, la déchéance devient valeur humaine' (p. 187).

This survival of the victim's humanity is supplemented, for Perec, by the writing of the survivor's testimony, which can work on the mass of experience, 'tour à tour machinerie énorme ou quotidien lamentable', to produce 'une cohérence, qui unisse et hiérarchise les souvenirs, et donne à l'expérience sa nécessité'; and this 'pour que son retour ait un sens, pour que sa survie devienne victoire' (p. 188). The literary context of Perec's piece is vital here if we are to understand the force of his argument. The essay on Antelme was the fourth and last of a series of pieces written for the review *Partisans*; in the preceding texts, Perec had set out his critique of the prevailing tendencies in French literary thought. These were represented by, on the one hand, Sartrean *engagement*; on the other, associated by Perec with such names as Blanchot, Paulhan and, more recently, Robbe-Grillet, a refusal of the referential capacity of literature in favour of self-conscious meditations on the limits of expression.[4] Sartre's position had admirable aims, but was aesthetically superficial; the alternative preoccupation with the 'crisis of language' amounted to irresponsibility. The task, then, would be to find a literature which could honour its obligation to engage with the world, while also fulfilling its specifically literary function by realizing this engagement in a process of formal re-elaboration. And this is what Perec finds in Antelme.

His essay on *L'Espèce humaine* opens with criticism of a false opposition: between the inexpressible world of the concentration camps and 'la "vraie" littérature'. 'L'on ne sait pas très bien', writes

Perec, 'si c'est la littérature que l'on méprise, au nom des camps de concentration, ou les camps de concentration au nom de la littérature'. In any case, the supposed distinction is refused on principle: 'Toute expérience ouvre à la littérature et toute littérature à l'expérience' (p. 174). But the specific question remains: how to write? 'Il s'agit de témoigner de ce que fut l'univers concentrationnaire. Mais qu'est-ce qu'un témoignage?' (p. 175).

The survivor, according to Perec, finds a facile, pseudo-acceptance of what he has to say, which serves in fact to deny his witness: 'on ne cherche ni à comprendre, ni à approfondir' (p. 175). Against this context, Antelme provides an example of the literary elaboration of lived experience, re-articulated in specific form so that it might communicate:

Pour nous rendre sensibles à l'univers concentrationnaire, c'est-à-dire pour faire de ce qui l'avait atteint lui, quelque chose qui pourrait nous atteindre, et pour que son expérience particulière s'épuise dans la nôtre, Robert Antelme élabore et transforme, en les intégrant dans un cadre littéraire spécifique [...], les faits, les thèmes, les conditions de sa déportation. (p. 177)

It is this re-articulation that makes *L'Espèce humaine* a text of insurmountable importance for Perec. For only the properly aesthetic work of re-organization and questioning can make experience meaningful, can refuse to let it congeal into a symbol whose interpretation would be given in advance, and which can therefore be comfortably assimilated. 'Mais dans *L'Espèce humaine*, le camp n'est jamais donné. Il s'impose, il émerge lentement' (p. 178). The value of Antelme's testimony thus derives from his determination to work through his experiences—not therapeutically, but aesthetically and intellectually, and in order to engage his reader in the process: 'entre son expérience et nous, il interpose toute la grille d'une découverte, d'une mémoire, d'une conscience allant jusqu'au bout' (p. 178).

Far from an obstacle to communication, and contrary to the assumptions of a naïve understanding of testimony, this mediating 'grill' is the very condition of communication, allowing the sense of the experiences recounted to become apparent: 'Il n'y a pas d'*explications*. Mais il n'est pas un fait qui ne se dépasse, ne se transforme, ne s'intègre à une perspective plus vaste. L'événement, quel qu'il soit, s'accompagne toujours de sa prise de conscience: le monde concentrationnaire s'élargit et se dévoile' (p. 179). The ensemble of techniques used to assure this constant re-elaboration constitutes the link in Perec's analysis between Antelme's testimonial authenticity and his literary value. As 'des méthodes spécifiques de la création littéraire, en tant qu'elles sont organisation d'une matière sensible, invention d'un style, découverte d'un certain type de relations entre les éléments du récit, hiérarchisation, intégration, progression', these techniques 'brisent l'image immédiate et inopérante que l'on se fait de la réalité concentrationnaire': 'l'univers des camps apparaît pour la première fois sans qu'il nous soit possible de nous y soustraire' (pp. 179–80).

The ethical and the literary dimensions of Antelme's narrative are thus inseparable: the former are established only by the latter, on the basis of the work of re-interpretation imposed by this literary aspect on the reader. Perec is not understated in his assessment of the significance of Antelme's achievement: 'Cette transformation d'une expérience en langage, cette relation possible entre notre sensibilité et un univers qui l'annihile, apparaissent aujourd'hui comme l'exemple le plus parfait, dans la production française contemporaine, de ce que peut être la littérature' (p. 188). And against this achievement, he sets the contemporary avoidance of the world by a literature taking refuge in the fiction of the inexpressible, for which 'l'inexprimable est une valeur', in which 'on nous invite à lire entre les lignes cette inaccessible fin vers laquelle tout écrivain authentique se doit de tendre: le silence' (p. 188). But there is no escaping the world, says Perec. 'Nous n'avons pas d'autre vie à vivre' (p. 189). And this shabbily self-indulgent *faux*-pessimism is comprehensively belied by the work of transformation and re-articulation which constitutes *L'Espèce humaine*. Triumphantly, Perec declares: 'Nous pouvons dominer le monde. Robert Antelme nous en fournit l'irréfutable exemple' (p. 189). Returning to literature its lost meaning, Antelme restores a faith in language disguised by its current supposed 'crisis'—'le langage qui, jetant un pont entre le monde et nous, instaure cette relation fondamentale entre l'individu et l'Histoire, d'où naît notre liberté': 'À ce niveau, langage et signes redeviennent déchiffrables. Le monde n'est plus ce chaos que des mots vides de sens désespèrent de décrire. Il est une réalité vivante et difficile que le pouvoir des mots, peu à peu, conquiert' (p. 190). Which brings Perec to his wonderfully celebratory conclusion: 'Par son mouvement, par sa méthode, par son contenu enfin, *L'Espèce humaine* définit la vérité de la littérature et la vérité du monde' (p. 190).

It is impossible not to respond rather anxiously to the confidence of Perec's assertions. His redemptive references to domination, triumph and victory, his vocabulary of foundations and conquest, sit uneasily with his unparalleled sensitivity to the vulnerable, passive, fractured solidarity of the deportees. His insistence on the triumph of Antelme's text overrides the important sense in which this triumph is, for Antelme, always still to be accomplished, in the ongoing political refusal of injustice which alone could realize the sense of his testimony—and then, only as *contestation permanente*. As we have now seen more than once, Antelme's characteristic dialectic is not one of 'dépassement': rather, the values (the human, community) derived from their attempted negation return immediately to contest this negation, with no time to establish themselves as positive terms outside of this struggle. And the truth of his testimony, therefore, can only ever be a truth waiting to be realized, in the just response of unknown, ever-futural readers.

But Perec's reading nevertheless remains of immense importance, for two reasons: these concern, respectively, solidarity and testimony. First, and quite simply, his delicate tracing of Antelme's notion of eroded solidarity is without compare. Secondly, his account of the work done by Antelme's text actively to articulate his experiences serves as a vital corrective to any reading which would assimilate Antelme's testimony to a fascination with the irresolvable blockage produced by the encounter between the inexpressible and the demands of expression. Such readings pay attention to only the first paragraph-and-a-half of Antelme's 'Avant-propos', which gives this fascination ample material: 'dès les premiers jours cependant, il nous paraissait impossible de combler la distance que nous découvrions entre le langage dont nous disposions et cette expérience que, pour la plupart, nous étions encore en train de poursuivre dans notre corps'; 'A peine commencions-nous à raconter, que nous suffoquions. A nous-mêmes, ce que nous avions à dire commençait alors à paraître *inimaginable*' (*EH*, 9). But Antelme does not stop here; and his continuation is precisely what Perec has understood. 'Nous avions donc bien affaire à l'une de ces réalités qui font dire qu'elles dépassent l'imagination,' writes Antelme. 'Il était clair désormais que c'était seulement par le choix, c'est-à-dire encore par l'imagination que nous pouvions essayer d'en dire quelque chose' (*EH*, 9).[5]

Half a century after Antelme wrote these words, we are, for good reason, unaccustomed to thinking dialectically, let alone along the lines of so rigorously contestatory a dialectic as Antelme's. We prefer, perhaps, the static drama of paradox. Perec reminds us that Antelme does not.

Lyotard

In his *Heidegger et 'les juifs'*, Lyotard offers the following discussion of *L'Espèce humaine*:

Comparez Antelme et Wiesel, *L'Espèce humaine* et *La Nuit*. Deux représentations, certes. Mais Antelme résiste, c'est un résistant (*Espèce*, 95 sq., 131 sq., etc.). Toute résistance est ambiguë, comme son nom l'indique. Résistance politique, mais aussi résistance au sens freudien. Formation de compromis. Apprendre à négocier avec la terreur nazie, à la manœuvrer, même si c'est très peu. Essayer de la comprendre pour la déjouer. Jouer sa vie pour ça. Toucher les limites qui sont celles de l'espèce humaine, pour ça. C'est la guerre. La déportation est une partie de la guerre. Antelme sauve l'honneur.[6]

The contrast with Wiesel allows Lyotard to establish an opposition between Antelme's supposedly heroic resistance and the pernicious fiction of Jewish non-resistance, in order to dispute a model of heroism which, in valorizing virile resistance, facilitates the propagation of such fictions. The justice of this critique is beyond qualification. It may not be well served, however, by the choice of Antelme as counter-example. I will here follow up Lyotard's specific references to Antelme's text, in order to determine whether this characterization—which, plainly, pulls against the sense of the analyses offered in this study—is in fact exact.

The examples Lyotard cites from *L'Espèce humaine* concern, respectively, a visit by Antelme to the camp sickbay, and an extended discussion of the impossibility for the political prisoners in Gandersheim to occupy with any degree of effectiveness the camp's administrative structures. The second of these seems to make Lyotard's point: Antelme is discussing the continued possibility or otherwise of active resistance, and thereby does indeed extend the struggle into the world of deportation. But this is hardly a sufficient reading of the section in question. For this section is, in fact, Antelme's principal elaboration of the point made in his 'Avant-propos' (and so well glossed by Perec) regarding the impossibility of precisely such active, heroic resistance, and its necessary displacement into the vulnerability of individual exposure. If Antelme is indeed concerned to 'sauver l'honneur' (but whose? Lyotard does not specify. Members of the Resistance?

All political deportees? All deportees except the 'droit commun'? All deportees?), then he is doing so in a way which imposes a rethinking of what 'honour' might mean, here: in the sense, strangely, of Lyotard's own analysis.

The early paragraphs of this section make Lyotard's conclusions perhaps understandable. Antelme maintains the discourse of a political prisoner, and of the solidarity which might be expected amongst comrades in the camp: the 'Lagerältester' Paul, for example, is criticized for appointing his lover 'Et...' (a 'droit commun') as 'Stubendienst' in preference to the 'politique' Gilbert: 'Paul n'avait nullement le comportement d'un détenu politique'; 'Par ce premier acte, notre situation était gravement compromise'; 'Si notre kommando a pris l'allure qui apparaît à travers ce récit, si ce qu'on y a connu a été tout différent de ce qui était à Buchenwald par exemple, la cause en fut d'abord dans ce premier acte du lageraltester' (*EH*, 132–3). But read on: Antelme is here establishing the reasons for the erosion of conventional solidarity in Gandersheim, as indicated by his reference to Buchenwald, with its implicit distinction between Antelme's account and Rousset's. The model of active solidarity is therefore presented—Gilbert 'remplissait son rôle de détenu politique', the position of Kapo 'pour un politique devait surtout comporter des responsabilités à l'égard des camarades détenus' (p. 133)—in order for its impossibility to be appreciated: 'Ainsi ce qui était possible dans les camps où l'appareil était tenu par les détenus politiques ne devait pas l'être ici' (p. 134). It is, therefore, after this introduction that Antelme sets out his theorization of the impossibility of active solidarity, which we have seen above: 'Mais l'oppression et la misère étaient telles que la solidarité entre tous les politiques se trouvait elle-même compromise. Elle existait entre des groupes de trois, quatre copains. Mais, pour organiser, pour penser, il faut encore avoir de la force et du temps' (p. 135).

And yet the political prisoners nevertheless try to organize: so perhaps Lyotard is right, after all?

En dépit de cet ensemble de conditions, nous avions essayé de nous grouper autour de Gilbert. Des noyaux avaient été formés: renseignements, liaisons, action. Seuls quelques responsables étaient informés du rôle qu'ils auraient à tenir. Ce regroupement avait un double but: d'abord tenter d'assurer la sécurité des politiques qui pouvaient, à l'occasion de bagarres, être menacés par les droit commun; surtout, suivre de près la marche de la guerre et essayer de se préparer à une action au moment de l'approche des alliés. (p. 135)

'C'est la guerre. La déportation est une partie de la guerre. Antelme sauve l'honneur.' But again, it is as if Lyotard has read the first part of Antelme's exposition, without noticing the subsequent commentary: 'Mais cette tentative, elle aussi, devait échouer. L'opposition conjuguée du lageraltester et des kapos était trop forte, la misère du corps aussi' (*EH*, 135–6). 'Antelme sauve l'honneur'? Only if his point is that, honourably, they tried but failed. But this is not his point.

The key here is in Antelme's reference to 'la misère du corps'. In the following paragraphs (which we have considered above), Antelme discusses the fragmentation of solidarity, the reduction of a collective, resistant consciousness to a solitary struggle to survive, concluding: 'Mais quoique solitaire, la résistance de cette conscience se poursuivait. Privé du corps des autres, privé progressivement du sien, chacun avait encore de la vie à défendre et à vouloir' (p. 136). Ringing out at the end of a section, these last two sentences seem to appeal to a model of active heroism, maintained in the struggle of the individual will. But this would represent a highly selective reading, separating such affirmative moments from the complications with which, as seen in Chapter 2 above, they are insistently entwined in Antelme's account. Here, for example, we would have to forget that the individual who continues to will his own survival does so inasmuch as his body is gradually slipping away from him, which cannot but undercut this will with the pathos of its insufficiency. It is not that there is no agency here: again, as seen in Chapter 2 above, it is that this agency is both maintained and eroded, is thought of as residual. Throughout *L'Espèce humaine*, it is therefore amply clear that the struggle to survive is understood not simply at the level of the will, but also, dialectically and primarily, at the level of present suffering, and is therefore not understandable in terms of heroic activity.

It is perhaps not surprising that Lyotard's reading misses these complications: as a reading, it is markedly rapid, highlighting two sections (along with his empty, catch-all 'etc.') which he interprets selectively, and which, when considered more attentively, reveal his neglect of those aspects of Antelme's account which are not simply assimilable within this supposed active heroism. The first of his examples is, if anything, even more problematic for his analysis than the second.

In this section, Antelme visits a friend in the camp sickbay. The man he has come to see is not as ill as many; next to him, however, another prisoner is dying. Antelme's accompaniment of his friend is thus displaced, as this friend's protestations of his defiant survival ring out against the background of his neighbour's agony, in a painful counterpoint:

Le moribond gémit. On entend son souffle. Le copain cesse de parler. Il jette un coup d'œil sur le lit voisin, me le désigne de la tête et dit: 'Ils peuvent bien nous faire tous crever, ils l'ont dans le cul. Mais moi, ils n'auront pas ma peau. Je l'ai toujours dit, je rentrerai'. L'autre se tord sur sa paillasse; sa figure ruisselle. Ils ont l'air d'avoir eu la sienne. (p. 97)

This defiance is extremely difficult, however: for while it sounds overbearing next to his neighbour's agony (as suggested by Antelme's dry, melancholy 'Ils ont l'air d'avoir eu la sienne'), it also constitutes a refusal of the regime which has killed this neighbour. Antelme's juxtaposition thus both produces a clash between these two elements (defiance and agony) and relates them, the defiance coming to stand with the dying neighbour even as it jars against his last, exhausted moments:

La plainte du moribond augmente. Derrière la cloison trois ou quatre types continuent à chanter. L'odeur de l'urine se mêle à la plainte, à la chanson. Le type se tord atrocement. Sa figure fond, ses yeux noirs sont comme noyés. Le copain me dit lentement à voix basse: 'Un jour ça viendra tu sais, ils seront écrasés, tu comprends, écrasés'. (p. 97)

As the smell of urine bridges the gap between the dying man and others around him, a kind of solidarity is implied which, eroded, is composed of indifference and disharmony, as well as of friendship and care. The rhetoric of defiant solidarity used by Antelme's 'copain' (to which Lyotard reduces the passage as a whole) is thus qualified (but not dismissed) by its insertion into this wider weave of suffering and eroded solidarity. The rhythms of the prisoners' life take in such moments as this, cannot but do so; which means that this present suffering is both assimilated and remains as a scandal, punctuates and punctures these rhythms, affirms the existence and marks the slippages of solidarity, as Antelme's syntax implies:

Celui-là est mort. Ses copains s'en apercevront particulièrement, mais l'oublieront vite. Ça ne fait pas de bruit, rien ne s'arrête. Il meurt, c'est l'appel, il meurt, c'est la soupe, il meurt, on reçoit des coups, il meurt seul. (p. 100)

'Antelme sauve l'honneur.'

Lyotard's reading is not simply wrong. *L'Espèce humaine* cannot be understood without reference to the heroic, active solidarity it presents as still fully possible elsewhere. But, reducing Antelme's text to this model, this reading is certainly deficient. It ignores Antelme's mobilization of the remnants of this model, his critical displacement of its heroism into a residual resistance interspersed with, but no longer thinkable simply as, activity. What Lyotard misses is, oddly, marked in his 'etc.': all the rest, all the elaboration of Antelme's analysis through passages which seek to give the questions they raise full and careful treatment, not to neglect notions with which this analysis is in tension, but to situate them specifically and attentively. Too quick to schematize, what Lyotard misses is the writing of Antelme's testimony.

Notes to Readings (II)

1. Philippe Lejeune, *La Mémoire et l'oblique: Georges Perec autobiographe* (Paris: P.O.L., 1991), 117. See also David Bellos, *Georges Perec: A Life in Words* (London: Harvill, 1993), 449.
2. *EH*, 11; see Lejeune, *La Mémoire*, 115–16.
3. Georges Perec, 'Robert Antelme ou la vérité de la littérature', *TI*, 173–90 (181). On the apparent reasons for Perec's enthusiastic response to *L'Espèce humaine*, see Bellos, *Georges Perec*, 276–80; and, with care, Dan Stone's occasionally erroneous 'Perec's Antelme', *French Cultural Studies* 10/2 (June 1999), 161–72.
4. These pieces are collected in Georges Perec, *L.G. Une aventure des années soixante* (Paris: Seuil, 1992). On *Partisans*, see also Bellos, *Georges Perec*, 274–7.
5. Although the versions of Blanchot and Kofman through which he makes this case are considerable over-simplifications, Stone is therefore right to stress that Perec's Antelme is on the side of expression, not the ineffable.
6. Jean-François Lyotard, *Heidegger et 'les juifs'* (Paris: Galilée, 1988), 53.

CHAPTER 3

❖

Testimony

In its 1957 republication, *L'Espèce humaine* is designated a 'récit'. This designation persists in subsequent reprints of the 'Collection Blanche' edition, but is missing from the 'Tel' version. Just what kind of book is this?

Perhaps surprisingly, such a question is by no means out of place here. *L'Espèce humaine* is a carefully constructed text, which pays considerable attention to the important issue of its own status; moreover, the dialectic of resistance uncovered in Antelme's understanding of humanity is worked through in the detailed strategies of his writing. Whereas it has become something of a commonplace to remark upon the relative lack of stylistic adornment in the narrative of *L'Espèce humaine*, and to cite this supposed transparency as evidence of testimonial authenticity, I will be trying to show that, on the contrary, Antelme's text engages its substantial thematic considerations within the fabric of its composition; and that, moreover, the status of the text, and the respective roles of author and reader, are matters of urgent concern to Antelme as he elaborates his testimony.

This concern for the fate of his text as testimony presents the third strand of Antelme's strange, belated appeal to our contemporary context. A generalized fascination for testimony of all kinds, from the intimate to the world historical, is one of the striking features of contemporary Western culture, both intellectual and popular; and whether we privilege the authenticity offered (and occasionally placed in question) by the testimonial genre, or dwell on the consequences of such questioning for the possibility of such authenticity, Antelme's approach to these matters has proved especially resonant. I will be arguing that Antelme's understanding of testimony resonates with aspects of more recent trauma theory, as well as with the problematization of the opposition between the fictional and the testimonial; but also, that his model relies on a faith in authentic witness and communication which might trouble certain more recent positions.

Untimely in these two senses (as both forerunner and throwback), Antelme stages, in a way that is perhaps unique, the inevitable dislocation of the witness—while also mobilizing this dislocation, to insist on the necessity—the responsibility—to communicate.

In this chapter, accordingly, I will first consider Antelme's conception of testimony, examining in particular its temporality, its relation to the self, and its dialectic of truth and artifice. Subsequently, I will discuss the literary qualities of his narrative, looking in detail at the literary fabric of his text, and his meditations on the status of language during and after the experience of the camps. Throughout, it will be important to bear the following in mind: this area, the question of testimony, bears the full weight of those already examined in this study. If his testimony fails, disappears, is dismissed or ignored, none of Antelme's thinking in relation to humanity or community will be of the slightest significance.

(Future)

Considering the essential temporality of testimony, Dori Laub, a psychoanalyst engaged in the treatment of trauma survivors, and co-founder of the Video Archive for Holocaust Testimonies at Yale University, stresses above all its belatedness. This belatedness is three-fold: for at the time of its occurrence, the traumatic event cannot be grasped as such by those who experience it, cannot be known in its historical significance, and cannot be communicated to others.[1] The jolts of this delay are clear from Antelme's testimony: in his 'Avant-propos', and in the scenes at Dachau between the newly liberated prisoners and the American soldiers, Antelme stresses the prisoners' shock at the apparent ungraspability of their own experience. In response to this estrangement, the belatedness of testimony conse-quently becomes an essential part of Antelme's view of the nature of what he is writing. Specifically, he presents his account as a call to its reader, within the time of whose reading its meaning can be affirmed. In an initial sense, the testimony must be received in order to exist as such; part of the sense of this situation is that the reading of the testimony will realize the desired recognition of survival which its author recalls. On the march away from Gandersheim, and hard after his exposition of his central thesis, Antelme writes:

La guerre finit. On ne sait pas si je suis vivant. Mais je voudrais que l'on sache que, ce matin, je suis dedans, que je l'ai remarqué, que ma présence dans ce matin laisse des traces indiscutables et transmissibles. (*EH*, 233)

As it is read, the wish is realized: the 'traces' of Antelme's surviving presence are affirmed in the reader's acceptance of his testimonial authenticity. And it is no accident that these lines are placed within pages of Antelme's most explicit theorization of the indivisibility of humanity: for the recognition of these traces is also an affirmation of the human as irreducible residue, against the impossible Nazi desire for complete annihilation. To this extent, the survivor is also a trace of all those who have not survived, and the confirmation of his testimony in its reading also contests the order which has put them to death, forming a space within which, in defiance of this desire, the traces of their common suffering are marked.

The reader thus becomes the space into which the memory of the survivor—and, through his communication of this memory, the trace of those who have not survived—is transmitted, the just 'Moi–Sujet' welcoming and guarding the humanity whose threatened abolition the testimony records. The reader is, accordingly, a particular locus of a wider historical operation, in which the irreducible traces of the victims will refute the logic of their murderers. As we have seen, Antelme argues forcefully that the Nazis 'ne peuvent pas non plus enrayer l'histoire qui doit faire plus fécondes ces cendres sèches que le gras squelette du lagerführer' (p. 79). Here we have, to anticipate a little, a hint of the writerly delicacy with which Antelme's text is composed: 'histoire' here indicates not only the historical dimension within which this refutation will take place, but the narrative which allows this to happen—this narrative, then, and my reading of it, now. This prediction is thus also a demand: for a reading which will, to use Antelme's image, be fertilized by these ashes, ensuring the affirmation of the irreducible humanity they declare.

Both on his own account, and in the name of those others who have not survived, Antelme's testimony calls to its reader (from his own milieu and elsewhere: the reference to 'cendres' is, we should again note, Antelme bearing witness to a suffering which is not his own; the implications of this move for his understanding of testimony will be discussed below). The reader is asked not only to realize the testimony simply by reading it (the generic demand of testimony as such): the untimely community of text and reader is to become the space within which a specific ethics can be elaborated, honouring the memory of the victims of the concentrationary regime, whether they have survived or not, by refusing its logic. The reader is not asked to empathize with the sufferings described: rather, she is called to house the memory of these sufferings, in a gesture of accompaniment which also affirms an inevitably fractured solidarity against the violence of their infliction. Antelme himself, as reader, sketched the nature and the import of this gesture in his response to Blanchot's *L'Ecriture du désastre*:

Le mouvement de reconnaissance de l'autre, de l'autre infini, nature de cette pensée — sa servitude: le genre humain jamais abandonné. Pensée accompagnée, elle porte l'ombre de l'autre, elle serait le silence, la 'parole muette' du lecteur. (*TI*, 67)

While it is far from clear that the role to which Antelme's reader is called should be seen as redemptive in relation to the suffering she is asked both to recognize and to contest (we will have to return to this question below), it is the case that the affirmative position she is asked to occupy corresponds to what we might view as the potentially healing function of organized, written testimony. Just as the reader can become the space in which the witness's testimony and survival can be realized and confirmed, so can the writing of testimony be considered a process of integration, in which ownership may gradually be taken of the traumatic experience which escaped its victim in the time of its occurrence. The goal of such a process is what Lawrence Langer has called 'cotemporality': the attempt to reconstruct a kind of existential continuity, within which memories of trauma might form a part of the overall narrative of a life.[2] *L'Espèce humaine* has been seen as the kind of memoir which could facilitate such a process of integration: Colin Davis, in particular, reads it as the affirmation of the surviving existential self, the ability still to say 'I' after the threatened abolition of this self, and sees the apparent closure of the text as symptomatic of this restorative story.[3] There is certainly a clarity to Antelme's prefatory qualification, 'Je rapporte ici ce que j'ai vécu' (*EH*, 11): not only the careful restriction of the account to that witnessed by its author (from which Antelme does occasionally depart, however, as will be considered below), but also the sense that what follows is the account of a lived experience which has, by implication, been existentially assimilated. Antelme stresses that the experience carried on after the deportees' return; but this continuation is situated in the past, as 'cette expérience que, pour la plupart, nous étions encore en train de poursuivre dans notre corps' (p. 9). What follows, Antelme seems to say, is the story of part of my life: the life of this 'Je' who is speaking to you, now, in this 'Avant-propos'. It would seem fair, therefore, to view the position from which this preface is written as one of the accomplishment of Langer's 'cotemporality'.[4]

Langer emphasizes, however, that such accomplishment is experienced primarily as a goal, an 'impossible task'.[5] And this narrative of healing must, indeed, be disrupted: Antelme's letter to Mascolo, from June 1945, whose ghostly imagery we have already considered in Chapter 1 above, introduces a moment of discontinuity within its therapeutic flow. As we have seen, Antelme anticipates with unease the process of healing: he writes that 'je recommence à me ressembler', that 'Tous mes amis m'accablent avec une satisfaction pleine de bonté, de ma ressemblance avec moi-même'.[6] The purpose of his remarks, however, is to insist that the otherness he has experienced will infiltrate the supposed process of integration, displacing the returning old self from within; and that the knowledge of this persisting internal non-coincidence is all that makes the healing process bearable: 'Alors peut-être j'accepterai la ressemblance avec moi-même parce que je saurai qu'elle n'est pas'.[7]

But this is not *L'Espèce humaine*. Mascolo tells us that Antelme's letter was written from a 'maison de repos' at Amblainvilliers, and that the composition of *L'Espèce humaine* did not begin until the return from a visit to Elio and Gina Vittorini in Italy in summer 1946.[8] It may be, perhaps, that we must again distinguish between these two testimonial instances, and see *L'Espèce humaine*, with its apparent closure and existential integration, as symptomatic of the healing uneasily anticipated in the letter to Mascolo. What Antelme regrets in this letter is what he calls the 'heavenly' period during which he was able to deliver himself of his testimony in its most immediate form; with this text in mind, it is difficult not to read *L'Espèce humaine* as the transcendence of this period, an act of mediate communication produced from a position of recovery.[9]

On the other hand, it is difficult to rest easy with this reading: it may be that the internal non-coincidence which Antelme hopes to incorporate within himself is also marked within his testimony, despite the apparent wholeness of the self who speaks in the 'Avant-propos'. This would suggest the approach discussed in the above account of Blanchot's reading of the text, privileging the loss of self suggested in Antelme's testimony, rather than its persistence; and the letter to Mascolo has indeed been deployed as evidence in such a reading.[10] And it might be necessary to develop the implications of this unease a little further: if the narrative of healing apparently indicated by Antelme's 'Avant-propos' is to some extent disrupted by his anticipatory fear of this outcome, perhaps the communication of testimony is similarly precarious?

Belatedness imposes its own pathos, of course. Not only has the event which compels testimony escaped the comprehension of the witness; the reception of this testimony, the time and space in which it is meaningfully realized, similarly escapes, receding into an always ungovernable future. This is why Derrida, for example, stresses the radical emptiness of the future of testimony in his reading of Celan; or why Shoshana Felman and Lawrence Langer both use the image of an uncertain harbour to figure the risks entailed in the unpredictability of reception.[11] Antelme's wish that the traces of his presence be 'indiscutables' (EH, 233) is thus only ever that: it may be realized, as we affirm both his survival and the sense of his testimony in the time of our reading—but this affirmation might not happen, his testimony might be ignored or disputed, its sense radically altered by some future revelation. In Derridean terms, such uncertainty is also what makes testimony possible at all: it is the gap which, as the condition of possibility of communication, also cuts this communication through with the possibility of failure. As Blanchot and Lyotard have both observed, an insistence on the firm possibility of communication is marked as much by the strength of its desire as by the security of its fulfilment.[12] That silence, as Primo Levi suggests, is also a form of communication, and communication thus inevitable cannot quite be turned around into a guarantee that one's own signals will necessarily be transmitted successfully. One always does communicate; this is not the same as communication always being possible, within one's power.[13] If we have to choose between communication and non-communication, then yes, we must choose the former; this does not mean that such a choice is guaranteed a successful outcome.

When the American soldiers enter Dachau at the end of April 1945, their arrival is strikingly presented by Antelme as marked by several moments of failed communication. In particular, attempts at communication between the soldiers and those they have liberated tend to fail, as the testimony of the prisoners cannot be received by those who form their first audience: 'Le soldat, d'abord écoute, puis les types ne s'arrêtent plus: ils racontent, ils racontent, et bientôt le soldat n'écoute plus.' Antelme suggests the incapacity of the soldiers to imagine the horrors recounted in these stories, capturing this in the inadequacy of their language: 'C'est effroyable, oui, vraiment, ces Allemands sont plus que des barbares! *Frightful, yes, frightful!* Oui, vraiment, effroyable' (*EH*, 301). The flat translation of the soldiers' understandably inadequate response undercuts its attempted empathy with the impossibility of this gesture; pathetically, testimony falls at the first hurdle. And the prisoners become aware of this failure, in the face of the soldiers' ignorance, their own experience suddenly appearing to them in all its incommunicability:

Certains hochent la tête et sourient à peine en regardant le soldat, de sorte que le soldat pourrait croire qu'ils le méprisent un peu. C'est que l'ignorance du soldat apparaît, immense. Et au détenu sa propre expérience se révèle pour la première fois, comme détachée de lui, en bloc. Devant le soldat, il sent déjà surgir en lui sous cette réserve, le sentiment qu'il est en proie désormais à une sorte de connaissance infinie, intransmissible. (p. 301)

The traumatic event may start to be owned by its victim in the process of testimony; but this process also, here, reveals this event as incommunicable, a 'connaissance infinie' which also seems, as Delbo terms it, 'inutile'.

The two ends of Antelme's text join together at this point, as the celebrated description in his 'Avant-propos' of the prisoners' experience on their return extends this initial awareness of incommunicability beyond the world of the camps, and into their recognition as survivors and, thus, witnesses. The physical 'traces' of their ordeal are experienced as an insufficient representation, and the desire emerges to supplement these with oral testimony: 'nous ramenions avec nous notre mémoire, notre expérience toute vivante et nous éprouvions un désir frénétique de la dire telle qu'elle' (*EH*, 9). This proves impossible, however, as the gap between their experience and the language in which this might be described turns out to be unbridgeable. As we saw in 'Readings (II)' above, Antelme writes: 'A peine commencions-nous à raconter, que nous suffoquions. A nous-mêmes, ce que nous avions à dire commençait alors à nous paraître *inimaginable*' (p. 9).

Antelme has no intention, however, of remaining with this simple opposition between communication and non-communication. Unlike Levi on the one hand, and those, on the other, who insist on the radical unrepresentability of the *univers concentrationnaire*, he does not posit an all-or-nothing choice between communication and silence: in his characteristically dialectical fashion, he has set up the impossibility of communication in order to formulate the true nature of its possibility, which is not opposed to this impossibility, but rather must be thought in and against its inevitability. Like Levi, he will not accept the option of 'incommunicability': the notion that the experiences of the victims of the camps are simply 'unimaginable' is too easy, he argues, too comfortable, a refusal to encounter the demands made by these experiences on the victims' audience: '*Inimaginable*, c'est un mot qui ne divise pas, qui ne restreint pas. C'est le mot le plus commode. Se promener avec ce mot en bouclier, le mot du vide, et le pas s'assure, se raffermit, la conscience se reprend' (p. 302). Italicizing them both, Antelme draws together the uses of the term 'inimaginable' at the beginning and the end of his text; the second instance argues that the first (which, we should remember, described the situation of the survivors in relation to their own experience) is also insufficient. Insufficient, perhaps, because an acceptance of this situation by the survivor will, as Perec suggests, allow his audience to miss the sense of his testimony, to walk on past the scandal of suffering: 'La plupart des consciences sont vite satisfaites et, avec quelques mots, se font de l'inconnaissable une opinion définitive. Alors, ils finissent par nous croiser à l'aise, se faire au spectacle de ces milliers de morts et de mourants' (p. 302).[14]

If this ease is to be challenged, Antelme argues, the incommunicable will have to be communicated. But not just by insisting on its communicability; rather, by working it through the resources of communication, using the imagination to express the unimaginable. This is Antelme's negotiation of the problem of artifice in testimonial reconstruction: characteristically, he refuses to set artifice and truthfulness against each other, instead making artifice a condition of truthfulness. If the soldiers use the unimaginability of the survivors' stories as a shield against their horror, this is because these stories are indeed told 'telles qu'elles', lacking the element of presentation necessary for their truth to be receivable:

Les histoires que les types racontent sont toutes vraies. Mais il faut beaucoup d'artifice pour faire passer une parcelle de vérité, et, dans ces histoires, il n'y a pas cet artifice qui a raison de la nécessaire incrédulité. Ici, il faudrait tout croire, mais la vérité peut être plus lassante à entendre qu'une fabulation. (p. 302)[15]

Antelme is not recommending invention: this conclusion would be possible only on the basis of an opposition between truth and artifice.

Rather, he is making a point which, half a century later, remains both current and difficult to accept: that testimonial authenticity depends, to be receivable, upon the structures of fiction implied in the business of reconstruction. Rather than simply emphasizing this inextricability, lamenting it, or exploiting it for the purposes of revisionism and bad faith, Antelme proceeds to insist that it be thought dialectically. The third moment in his thought (after the necessity and the impossibility of testimony) is, accordingly, the following (which, again, we met briefly in 'Readings (II)' above):

Cette disproportion entre l'expérience que nous avions vécue et le récit qu'il était possible d'en faire ne fit que se confirmer par la suite. Nous avions donc bien affaire à l'une de ces réalités qui font dire qu'elles dépassent l'imagination. Il était clair désormais que c'était seulement par le choix, c'est-à-dire encore par l'imagination que nous pouvions essayer d'en dire quelque chose. (p. 9)

In terms of his approach to testimony, I would suggest that Antelme's importance to a contemporary readership lies in the structure of this thought. The relation he establishes between possibility and impossibility, between testimony and fiction, truth and artifice, is close enough to the problematization of these oppositions to interest contemporary audiences fascinated by aporia; and yet he retains something else, some specificity not quite exhausted by this interest.[16] The difference, again, is the dialectic: the fact that, while Antelme's thought might seem to be working with a model of inextricability, it is actually organized by a threefold movement which is as distinct from this contemporary thought as it is, in fact, idiosyncratic. In this instance, the third term which Antelme posits is the production of testimony through and against its own impossibility; as we have seen, the characteristic move of Antelme's thought is for this third term to refuse transcendence, doubling back immediately as the contestation of the situation in which it has been produced. In the case of humanity, the negation of the human reveals its own negation —but this is also its immanent contestation, not its victorious transcendence; in the case of testimony, the unimaginable imposes the imagination as necessary—but in order to contest the situation which has produced the unimaginable. That Antelme's negation of the negation refuses transcendence is what makes his model resemble mutual implication (the inhuman within the human, the fictional within the testimonial); that this refusal operates in the name of the contestation of this first negation is what gives Antelme's thought a mobility and a minimal, residual agency incompatible with this aporia.

This refusal also lends Antelme's thought the fragility which constitutes much of its current appeal. That it implies no transcendence means that its contestation might always fail: the victim is not helped by the indestructibility of his humanity, the testimony might always be dismissed. For the reader of Antelme's testimony, this raises a particular set of questions. Is the time of my reading that of the emptiness of testimony, or its future realization? The affirmation or the pathos of its call for contestation? Most dramatically: can I consider my reading as in any sense the redemption of this testimony—or am I bound only to witness the impossibility, or even the failure of such redemption? In order to explore how these questions might be answered, we will now have to turn to an aspect of *L'Espèce humaine* which, I will argue, has rarely received the attention it deserves: quite simply, its writing.

'Débarrassé de toute littérature'

In his 'Hommage à Robert Antelme', published in *Le Monde* shortly after Antelme's death, Edgar Morin formulated succinctly what has become a widely held view of *L'Espèce humaine*, describing it as 'un chef-d'œuvre de littérature débarrassé de toute littérature'.[17] In the second half of his quasi-Blanchotian phrase, Morin is deploying the pejorative sense of 'littérature', as all that is artificial, insincere, showy, as in Verlaine's 'Et tout le reste est littérature'.[18] Overall, the view encapsulated in this formula is that which praises Antelme's testimony for its mostly straightforward lexis, its absence of self-consciously writerly tricksiness, its determination to present the world of the camps as directly as possible. While Morin is certainly right to highlight the generally anti-rhetorical style of Antelme's prose, this view of *L'Espèce humaine* represents both an underestimation of its writing strategies, and a misunderstanding of Antelme's theorization of the role of these strategies in relation to the testimonial function of his text. As we have seen, Antelme rejects the opposition between truth and artifice which makes possible the notion that his text might be free from all 'littérature': he insists, explicitly, that the artificial, the writerly, is necessary to the communication of the truth. And not just incidentally: 'il faut *beaucoup d'artifice* pour faire passer une parcelle de

vérité' (*EH*, 302; my emphasis). To worry that this undermines testimonial authenticity is to fail to follow Antelme in his dialectical
relation of the two terms, his thinking of truth through and against
artifice. Moreover, this situation is also dictated by 'cette disproportion
entre l'expérience que nous avions vécue et le récit qu'il était possible
d'en faire' (p. 9): there are no words adequate to this experience,
Antelme tells us so, there are only inadequate words worked in such a
way that they can nevertheless manage to convey something of its
truth. There is no adequation; but there is, for this very reason, the
possibility of articulation.

In this section, accordingly, I will be focusing on the literary and
self-conscious aspects of *L'Espèce humaine*, in order to correct this
widespread but reductive notion of its stylistic neutrality, and to
attempt to grasp some of the key elements of Antelme's approach to
the writing of his testimony. I will subsequently be discussing the role
of literary and cultural references in his text, and the meditations on
the value of language which run through it; first, however, in order to
provide some flavour of its literary texture, I propose to undertake a
close reading of what is arguably the high point of 'literariness' in
Antelme's testimony, namely the passage in which he recalls Good
Friday in Gandersheim (pp. 194–5).

This passage stands out from the rest of Antelme's testimony, as it
contains a strikingly denser deployment of figurative techniques,
stylistic variation, and so on, than that which characterizes his writing
elsewhere. I will discuss some of these shortly. First, though, we may
note that this section also presents a concentrated series of departures
from the strictly testimonial ethos of *L'Espèce humaine*, the
undertaking that 'je rapporte ici ce que j'ai vécu' (p. 11). As is often
the case, these departures are signalled by references to the ash of the
crematoria (explicitly absent from Gandersheim), of which there are
three, the first two making this departure absolutely clear: 'Toutes les
cendres sur la terre d'Auschwitz'; 'les tonnes de cendres d'Auschwitz';
'Silence des cendres épandues sur une plaine' (p. 195). There are also
references to soap made from human bodies, and human skin made
into lampshades, both of which indicate reference to a more broadly
understood concentrationary context than that of Gandersheim.
Some of the motivation for this is apparent in the pathos of the
reference to 'M.-L. A... morte, squelette, rasée', the initials understandable from the text's dedication as those of Antelme's sister,
Marie-Louise, arrested in the same raid as her brother, and who died

in Ravensbrück after the liberation of the camp. From the inclusion of this reference, we can understand more readily that when Antelme steps beyond his own testimonial context, he is doing what he elsewhere calls the reader to do: bearing witness for the witness, here, for those who did not return. In these cases, however, such references have a further effect: they wind through this passage a tone of angry elegy, which its stylistic techniques work to sustain.

In the first place, this passage is striking for its use of short, staccato sentences, often set as whole paragraphs, which import into its rhythm an imposing amount of silence, across which the phrases can then mournfully echo.[19] The paratactic rhythm is established in the following paragraph: 'Mais c'est le Vendredi saint. Un homme avait accepté la torture et la mort. Un frère. On a parlé de lui' (p. 195). While this paragraph establishes the thematic opposition which organizes the passage, between the Passion of Christ and the sufferings in the camps, it also sets up an abrupt rhythm which is then worked out across the following, which adds to it this tone of resonant lament:

> K... est mort, lui, et on ne l'a pas reconnu.
> Des copains sont morts en disant: 'Les vaches, les fumiers...'
> Les petits tziganes de Buchenwald asphyxiés comme des rats.
> M.-L. A... morte, squelette, rasée.
> Toutes les cendres sur la terre d'Auschwitz. (p. 195)

There is a gradual progression here: from Antelme's comrade K., whom he visited in the camp's makeshift sickbay, only to be devastated by his friend's unrecognizable appearance (see pp. 178–80), generalized to the death of 'des copains', then further to the 'petits tziganes de Buchenwald', and then away from Antelme's own context, but close within his heart, to Marie-Louise; and finally, out to the empty, tragic image of all the deaths, known or not, those for whom witness must be borne by proxy, 'toutes les cendres sur la terre d'Auschwitz'.

Around this use of parataxis as a rhythm of generalized mourning and protest, Antelme strings two strains of repetition, which provide a sense of unity again serving to set off the emptiness of these lines. The two terms which the text repeats are highlighted in an early sentence describing the story of the Passion: 'L'histoire d'un homme, rien que d'un homme, la croix pour un homme, l'histoire d'un seul homme' (p. 195). 'Histoire', it soon becomes clear, is used pejoratively in this case (rather as with 'littérature', above): the Passion is demoted to a 'Belle histoire', a 'Faible histoire, fluette, belle histoire dérisoire'

(p. 195), as the redeemed and redeeming sufferings of Christ are set against the urgent scandal of the camps. Again, though (as seen above in his reference to 'L'histoire qui doit faire plus fécondes ces cendres sèches', p. 79), Antelme allows the polysemy of 'histoire' to resonate, in two senses. First, it is 'histoire', in the sense of 'history', which separates the two orders of suffering invoked: because, reduced to a historical rather than a holy event, the Passion becomes just a 'story'; and because it is the historical nature of the sufferings of the camps that exacerbates them beyond redemption, insisting that they be understood and contested within historical, human time. Secondly, however, the derision directed at the mere 'story' of the Passion demands that this (which, as we have seen, is not simply direct, first-hand testimony) be understood as something else. Imaginative reconstruction, certainly (the references to Auschwitz can be nothing else, here); but not fiction. Rather: the dialectic of testimony; not a 'belle histoire', but a historical challenge to mourn and to act.

The second repeated term throughout this passage is 'homme'. The stakes of this repetition are clear: it insists on the exclusive humanity of Christ, thereby both refusing the redemptive dimension of his suffering, and affirming the indivisible humanity thematized elsewhere. This insistence also marks a polemical allusion to the Holy Family, contrasting with the 'enfants' at the end of the passage (the 'Hurlements des enfants que l'on étouffe' (p. 195): the little children, abandoned), calling to mind the connection between the Nativity and the Deposition: 'On ne donne pas les morts à leur mère ici' (p. 195). The Man of Sorrows, cradled by his mother at the foot of the Cross, the destiny prefigured in the same cradling of the Christ child, has the humanity which occupies the time between these two scenes underscored as a radical challenge to the divinity with which they are also endowed.

This kind of contrast, in which the Passion is set against the unredeeemed human suffering, here and now, in the camps, at times works into the pattern of Antelme's phrasing, as in the phrase which continues his challenge to the imagery of the Deposition with that of the Holocaust: 'Pas de traces de clous sur les abat-jour, seulement des tatouages artistiques' (p. 195). This dense, protesting juxtaposition is also bitterly ironic, in its choice of 'artistiques' to qualify the camp tattoos on the victims' skin; it is also, again, and intensely, dialectical. For this choice is itself artistic, selecting an inappropriate term to jar, and so to articulate its anger: but this is artistry as the communication of protest, not the skill of barbarity. As with his use of 'histoire',

Antelme implicates his own contestatory position in the detail of his writing.

The physical detail of this particular paragraph introduces a rapid, flowing, and balanced syntax ('on arrache l'or de leur bouche pour manger plus de pain, on fait du savon avec leur corps', p. 195), which presents it as a kind of summation of the protest found in the more paratactic sections above, a climax of anger and horror, set up in part by the rhythm of the passage as a whole. The section follows a clear and economical pattern: it opens with a setting of the scene at Gandersheim, the discussion of the Gospel; moves to Antelme's protesting humanization of the Gospel story, and then to his reflections on this story, when set against the sufferings of the camps. This structures the passage up to the line, 'Toutes les cendres sur la terre d'Auschwitz'; at this point, with the opening of the next paragraph ('La voix du copain passe'), the pattern is repeated, as discussion of the Passion leads to its representation as a moment of relative luxury, before concluding with the empty concentrationary landscape, 'Silence des cendres épandues sur une plaine'. Along with its use of repetition at the lexical level, this structural patterning provides the background against which the passage's anger— particularly, its mourning of specific losses, and the physical detail of its sufferings—emerges in relief.

Much of this passage's argument and characteristic style, and the relation between the two, are condensed in the version of Christ's cry from the cross which introduces its concluding sentence, in which Antelme cuts off Christ's words, offering only: 'Mon père, pourquoi m'avez-vous...' (p. 195). The argument of the passage here emerges in its implication that Christ can still speak, is still heard, is at least recognized as (in Antelme's terms) a human being: as Antelme puts it earlier in the passage, 'il peut dire des choses nouvelles et, si on le nargue, c'est qu'on est tenté du moins de le considérer comme quelqu'un' (p. 195). Its abbreviation indicates Antelme's separation of the story of the Passion from its redemptive symbolism, exaggerating the cry of despair by dislocating its familiar closure, emphasizing only its challenge to the supposedly omnipotent and benevolent God whose absence at moments of great suffering grounds not only the objections of non-believers, but also the perplexity of the faithful. Stripped in this way, the cry becomes just a human cry; but it is still too powerful for Antelme, as the comparisons made with other sufferings indicate. The use of ellipsis not only serves to abbreviate the phrase for the ends just described:

it also forces its juxtaposition with the fragments of names which are highlighted in the central, staccato section of the passage: 'K...' and 'M.-L. A...'. 'K...' died 'et on ne l'a pas reconnu': but in Christ's case, 'on est du moins tenté de le considérer comme quelqu'un'. 'M.-L. A... morte, squelette, rasée': but Christ 'a de la chair fraîche sur les os' (p. 195). The ellipsis which cuts off Christ's words thus enforces a reconsideration of Antelme's, taking the reader back through the whole of this passage to establish the contrast in sufferings which founds its argument. But we are also taken forward: for the words from the cross contrast with the diminuendo of the closing lines of this section: 'Hurlements des enfants que l'on étouffe. Silence des cendres épandues sur une plaine.' From an articulate cry of despair, through inarticulate terror to silence. But this silence is resonant: for it is mimed by the silence at the end of Antelme's section, into which these words resonate not as a cry of despair, but as a cry of anger, and a call to the reader. The silence of these ashes is also the time of the history which will come to make them fertile, the time of our reading, if we take up the challenge communicated through this series of careful textual devices.

The web of writerly techniques which Antelme uses to structure this particular passage implies a considerable faith in the ability of the literary, when serving the ends of testimony, to succeed in its aim of communicating the truth and the challenge of this testimony. Elsewhere in his text, however, when Antelme presents the role of literature or the arts in relation to the world of the camp, his position seems more ambivalent. Frequently, literary or cultural examples are introduced at scenes of uncertain communication, as if their own uncertain status in this environment were serving as a kind of synec-dochic intensification of the more general linguistic and cross-cultural hesitancies by which they are surrounded. During the enforced and inconsistent solidarity of the 'séance récréative' organized by Gaston, for example, the first performer is the nervous Francis, who recites sonnet 31 from Du Bellay's *Regrets* into a hum of continued conver-sation, the poem itself a tense rote performance seemingly isolated from its surroundings:

Heureux qui comme Ulysse a fait un beau voyage...
Il disait très lentement, d'une voix monocorde et faible.
— Plus fort! criaient des types au fond de la chambre.
... Et puis est retourné plein d'usage et raison ...
Francis essayait de dire plus fort, mais il n'y parvenait pas. [...] Jusqu'au bout il se tint raide, angoissé comme s'il avait eu à dire l'une des choses les

plus rares, les plus secrètes qu'il lui fût jamais arrivé d'exprimer; comme s'il avait eu peur que, brutalement, le poème ne se brise dans sa bouche. (p. 204)

The ambiguity of this description presents the poem as indeed rare, strangely clandestine in its new context, but suggests that its status here is otherwise indeterminate. The sad choice of this sonnet, which laments a lost Anjou home, and contrasts this lament with Ulysses' heroic homecoming, compounds its awkward pathos, until it is not at all clear whether any value (whether of nostalgia, escapism, encouragement or cultural self-affirmation) can be attached to its performance.[20] Similarly, when a German Kapo gropes for a scrap of French culture whilst ordering Antelme about his forced labour, it is impossible to discern the nature of their shared laughter:

> — *Los! Mensch, Arbeit!*
> Je sors lentement de la planque. Il me regarde avec ses petits yeux bleus. Il ne sait pas s'il doit gueuler encore.
> — *Franzose?*
> — *Ja.*
> Je marche à côté de lui, vers le talus. Il baisse la tête, puis la relève brusquement vers moi, comme illuminé:
> — *Ach!* Alexandre Dumas?
> — *Ja.*
> Il rigole et moi aussi. (pp. 51–2)

Their laughter perhaps comes from a moment of connection within their violent estrangement, or from the ridiculous presence of Dumas in this context, or the awfulness of Dumas ... all of these seem possible; as does the idea that the two might be laughing for entirely separate reasons, the one with delight at having rescued this long-forgotten name, the other with pleasure at the appearance of part of his culture here, or incredulity, or scorn for its triviality. The net effect appears to be that the ambivalence of the scene as a whole is condensed into the cultural reference which is its pivot.

This ambivalence is also in evidence within what is, overall, the unambiguously positive exchange between Antelme and the German evangelist, one of the text's high points of fractured solidarity, a rare 'moment of reprieve', in Primo Levi's terms.[21] Through his virtual incomprehension of the other's language, Antelme does manage to catch the word 'Musik', and the man's subject; but, again, its incongruity is extreme:

Dans ce marécage de langage, j'attrapais aussi parfois: *Musik, Musik*; il le prononçait comme l'auraient prononcé les SS. Il parlait de Mozart. Autour de nous, les copains étaient penchés sur leur atelier. Un meister foutait des coups de pied à un copain. Le compresseur crépitait. *Musik* résonnait dans la tête et couvrait le bruit de l'usine. (p. 75)

Incomprehension proves no barrier to connection, and this connection provides a heady escape from the violence by which it is surrounded; on the other hand, the cultural reference which has achieved this is also inextricable from this violence, as the entwining of Mozart's name with the accent of 'les SS' makes clear. This paragraph ends, moreover, with the failure of their attempt to communicate: 'Mozart' will not save them. But the name does provide an initial hint of contact, which is perhaps fulfilled in their subsequent shared enjoyment of a brief respite before the winter landscape. Again, the status of the cultural reference condenses that of the scene of communication in general, its hope and its impossibility, its optimism and its pathos.

These examples all possess an uncertainty which complicates further Antelme's conception of the role of the literary in relation to testimony. They suggest an insurmountable incongruity in the appearance of the literary (or, more broadly, the artistic) within the concentrationary world, which in turn leads to an irreducible ambiguity about their status in this world, especially regarding communication. As far as his general understanding of the role of literary artifice in testimony is concerned, however, Antelme holds firm to his dialectical belief in the possibility of communication through artifice. The two sides are not drawn into relation by Antelme, and it is not clear what we should make of this. On the one hand, we might read it as a simple discrepancy between two aspects of his thought. On the other hand, we might argue that the possibility of testimony is never more than possibility, can never guarantee successful communication, and thus that the role of the literary as staged within the text and its role as articulating factor in the text's transmission are strangely consonant, both offering the pathos of a gesture towards communication which cannot ensure its own fulfilment. But in any case, it seems that the literary, which for Antelme is essential to the communication of the truth of testimony, has a more ambivalent place when thematized within this testimony.

Perhaps a clearer sense of how to address this ambivalence might come from a consideration of Antelme's treatment of the question of language, since in this case, the dramatization of this question within the text is closer to the text's own approach. Frequently, as we will see, language is presented by Antelme as at least inadequate; but it is, as we might perhaps expect, through this inadequacy that its significance may be apprehended.

We have seen above the disproportion which for Antelme exists between the experience of the camps and the language in which this experience might be communicated, which becomes apparent as soon as the prisoners attempt to describe this experience to the American soldiers liberating Dachau. But something of the sort is already suggested at the point in the narrative at which news of the Allied advance over the Rhine reaches Gandersheim. The prisoners are now described as having acquired a new significance for their captors, namely that of their imminent defeat. But this altered relationship cannot be captured in words, since the relevant words cannot be uttered in the context of the camp:

Leur propre défaite vue à travers la victoire de ceux qu'ils appelaient *alles scheisse*, c'était insoutenable.

Mais nous ne leur crierions pas: 'Vous êtes écrasés'. Ils ne nous diraient pas: 'Vous mourrez parce que nous perdons la guerre'. Rien ne serait jamais dit. Les coups allaient tomber en silence. (p. 156; German as in original)

That Antelme chooses moments which are steps towards liberation to include reflections which have sceptical implications for his aim of communication suggests the extent to which he thinks this communication in all its complication. For, beyond its inability to grasp the suffering of the prisoners adequately, or to express their changing status at the end of the war, Antelme at times presents language as a positive danger within the camp, a temptation to be resisted:

Francis avait envie de parler de la mer. J'ai résisté. Le langage était une sorcellerie. La *mer*, l'*eau*, le *soleil*, quand le corps pourrissait, vous faisaient suffoquer. C'était avec ces mots-là comme avec le nom de M... qu'on risquait de ne plus vouloir faire un pas ni se lever. (p. 169)

The old words effect a link back to the old world which is too painful to be borne; and as such, they are to be avoided. ('M...', incidentally, is Marguerite Duras.) Or, alternatively: the old words represent, in their eroded continuation, a form of defiance; a small freedom, like pissing, a residual bodily persistence, a *shibboleth* of resistance: 'On aura toujours cette certitude, même méconnaissable pour les siens, d'employer encore ce même balbutiement de la jeunesse, de la vieillesse, permanente et ultime forme de l'indépendance et de l'identité' (p. 51). Antelme's impassioned attachment to his initial, oral testimony may perhaps be appreciated all the more in the light of these lines. And yet this might just be an illusion: as the later examples of disproportion and inadequacy suggest, the apparent continuation of language might just be a mirage, the trickery of a paleonym: 'C'est peut-être le langage qui nous trompe; il est le même là-bas qu'ici; nous nous servons des mêmes mots, nous prononçons les mêmes noms. Alors on se met à l'adorer car il est devenu l'ultime chose commune dont nous disposions' (p. 51). The 'dont nous disposions' returns us to the 'Avant-propos', where the same phrase is used to describe the inadequacy of the available language (see p. 9): it would seem that this early impression is indeed an illusion, and the gap between the old words and this new world would become more painfully apparent with time. This had already, in fact, been suggested by the twists to which German is subjected in the camp: 'Il restait cependant que ce langage faisait l'effet d'une trahison de tous les mots: *Scheisse, Schweinkopf*, loin de qualifier ici les SS, comme on aurait pu s'y attendre, n'y servaient plus qu'à les désigner, eux, Français' (p. 17).[22]

Language, then, is inadequate, and indicates the separation of the camp from the world outside, whose words no longer mean what they should, or are to be resisted because this meaning, in its intact beauty, is too painful, or are unable to describe the realities of the new universe into which they too have been dragged. Mostly, it is French which serves Antelme for these considerations, since it is the language which he has carried with him into the camp; the above German example is a relative rarity. But this example does in fact suggest how Antelme will approach this question of the unreliable, inadequate nature of language as a vehicle to communicate the experiences of the camps. For he does insist that communication is possible, both within the camps and across the boundary between camp and outside world; and the moments which make this suggestion tend to take place in German. For, typically, Antelme tackles the impossibility of communication dialectically: it is in the heart of communication's denial that communication takes place.

The thesis of the indivisibility of humanity is demonstrated most dramatically in the camps, Antelme argues, because it is here that the attempt to deny this indivisibility is at its most extreme. It is the lack of any substantial difference between victims and oppressors even 'dans le moment le plus fort de distance entre les êtres' (p. 229) that makes it possible and necessary to affirm the unity this moment seems to negate. It is, accordingly, across this distance that the possibility of communication is also affirmed, against the attempt to present a human relation of oppression as the sign of a species barrier. The majority of moments of successful communication in Antelme's text, in which this attempt is explicitly or implicitly contested, take place in the language in which the attempt is formulated, instilling an immanent revolt within barbarism. Where we might expect the continuation of communication, in French, Antelme dramatizes mostly problems; where we might expect its entire negation, he dramatizes success, and rebellion.

The stakes of this are clear, from *L'Espèce humaine* alone: German is overwhelmingly the language of abuse, violence, attempted de-humanization, all the *Scheisse!*, *Weg!*, *Los!*, and so on, which punctuate the text. Antelme makes clear elsewhere the extent to which this violence became, for him, welded to this language: in his 1945 piece 'Vengeance?', he writes of 'le malaise instantané que me provoqua récemment au cinéma, pendant la projection d'un vieux film allemand, l'audition de certaines tonalités de la langue où je retrouvais celles de nos kapos' (*TI*, 21). And yet, precisely because of this, it is in German that the order of the camp meets its most striking challenges. This technique insists on the impossibility of the very division which this order sought to realize, between true Germans and all others; one of its most poignant examples comes in the shared moment of respite between Antelme and the German evangelist, marked by the latter's '*Das ist ein schön Wintertag*' (*EH*, 76; German as in original). Other Germans also offer friendship, assistance or solidarity: notably the civilian supervisor of the prisoners' work in the factory, and a woman who also works there. The former approaches Antelme and Jacques one morning:

Il nous a regardé [*sic*] travailler un moment, sans expression. Puis il s'est approché et il a dit d'une voix calme, assez nette:
— *Langsam!* (lentement).
On s'est retourné vers lui comme s'il venait de déclencher un signal tonitruant. On l'a regardé sans rien répondre, sans faire le moindre signe de connivence. Lui aussi nous a regardés, il n'a rien dit d'autre. Il n'a pas souri, pas fait un clin d'œil. Il est parti.
Langsam! Ça suffisait bien.
Ce qu'il venait de dire suffisait à l'envoyer dans un camp et à en faire un rayé comme nous. Dire *langsam* à des gens come nous, qui sommes ici pour travailler et crever, cela veut dire qu'on est contre les SS. (p. 59)

The action of this civilian, whom Antelme subsequently calls 'le Rhénan', is complemented shortly afterwards by that of the German woman:

Sa figure se crispe. Elle me tend la main fermée.
— *Nicht sagen*, dit-elle à voix basse. (Il ne faut pas le dire.)
Je prends ce qu'il y a dans sa main.
— *Danke.*
C'est dur ce qu'il y avait dans sa main. Je serre, ça craque.
Sa figure se détend.
— *Mein Mann ist Gefangene.* (Mon mari est prisonnier.)
Et elle s'en va.
Elle m'a donné un morceau de pain blanc. (p. 65; German as in original)

It is vital to Antelme that these gestures remain just that: for their incompletion also signals their clandestinity, and hence their revolt. He reflects on these instances:

Comme ce qui est arrivé avec le Rhénan, ce qui est arrivé avec cette femme restera inachevé. [...] Il faudra se contenter de savoir. Mais la puissance de l'attention est devenue formidable. Les convictions se font sur des signes. *Nicht sagen, langsam*: par le langage je ne saurai d'eux jamais rien de plus.
  [...]
  Et on guettera, on flairera l'Allemand clandestin, celui qui pense que nous sommes des hommes. (pp. 65–6)

Again, as with his discussions of eroded solidarity, it is here the temporality of this gesture, the absence of a moment in which it might complete itself, that gives it its particular force for Antelme. Of necessity, moments of communication between prisoners of different nationalities are often incomplete because of their use of German as a medium: the prisoners are joined together by precisely what separates them. But this is not simply a tragic irony: it is a revolt, a challenge to this separation from within. The most luminous instance of this comes with the text's closing scene (as seen in Chapter 1 above, and discussed further in 'Ja'); this scene is anticipated at the start of the section entitled 'La Route', after the execution of four comrades who have declared themselves unable to walk. On his way to the toilet, Antelme sees a group of Russian prisoners charged with burying these four. Then:

Quand je suis arrivé aux chiottes, un autre Russe était en train de pisser. Au F. sur ma veste, il a vu que j'étais Français. Il s'est tourné vers moi et il m'a fixé dans les yeux:
— *Kamerad Kaput*, a-t-il dit doucement.
— *Ja.* (p. 219)

The symbolism of the toilets as a place of poor solidarity is again declared, as the Russian's gentle sympathy both effects a moment of communication and, in this sympathy and this communication, refuses the murderous order signified by the medium of this revolt. When, after the liberation of Dachau, the prisoners discover rather awkwardly the extent to which this medium has become part of them, they can accordingly afford not to be devastated by this: for their use of German has implied refusal of at least as much as complicity with the camp regime, and its overspill into this situation only allows this refusal to affirm its fulfilment: 'Ils essayent de dire en anglais que New York est beau, et ils le disent en allemand. Lorsque le soldat demande s'ils connaissent Paris, croyant répondre *yes*, ils disent *ja*. Alors les types rigolent un peu, et le soldat aussi' (p. 300).

Overall, then, language has a rather ambivalent place in *L'Espèce humaine*; part of this ambivalence, however, is precisely about whether or not this ambivalence should itself be counted as positive or productive. The limitations, dangers and inadequacies of language during the experience of the camps, and its insufficiencies afterwards, are thoroughly addressed by Antelme; but he also suggests that in and against these problems, the capacity for linguistic communication remains, indeed that it is through the linguistic medium which it has rendered problematic that the regime of the camps can in part be contested. Language cannot 'work', in the face of the experiences which here confront it; and yet it does, can and must work, communicating something of these experiences, and, in this, rejecting their supposed justification. Just as the literary appears through Antelme's testimony as both necessary and ridiculous, offering gestures which at best can never be sure of their success, so more broadly does language constitute a kind of unfinished medium, a web of halting movements towards contact which both succeed and fail, preserving both the force and the pathos of their uncertain connections.

Antelme's model of testimony is thus distinct from those of Blanchot or Lyotard, for example, who wish to preserve within testimony the space of the unrepresentable; nor is it quite that of Agamben, for whom the witness must ensure that the lacunae of his language bear witness for those who have not been able to do so.[23] Nor, alternatively, is it quite that of Derrida, for whom the fictional and the testimonial are inextricably mutually implicated, without this undecidable complication invalidating any given testimony.[24] Antelme too, as we have seen, wants his testimony to honour the memory of those who are unable to bear witness; and he also undertakes this task by elaborating this testimony *via* at times intricate textual artifice. But Antelme is distinguished by his demand for a double mobilization of the oppositions between language and silence, truth and artifice: first, that the testimony be written by the means of artifice in order for its truth to be communicated, against the silence which threatens it; secondly, that the reader realize this truth in the unknowable future time of reading.

There can be no question of the successful future redemption of the sufferings to which Antelme bears witness—this much is clear from the relentless fragility of the models of communication proposed by his testimony. Nor, however, can there be any question that I am not being called to confront this very question, to become the agent of that history which is to make fertile the ashes of those who did not survive.[25] Perhaps this, then, is the place of Antelme's reader: as the space within which his call resonates. Redemption, for Antelme, is never present: it is replaced by immanent contestation, or the call to a future affirmation which can never be guaranteed. But the text has been read, and the call has been heard. This is not redemptive; and to make it so would be to misunderstand the substance of the call. *L'Espèce humaine* can be affirmed only if we decide to affirm it; not as triumph, but as a permanent accompaniment of the suffering other as revolt against this suffering, 'le genre humain jamais abandonné' (*TI*, 67).

Notes to Chapter 3

1. Dori Laub, 'Bearing witness or the vicissitudes of listening' and 'An event without a witness: Truth, testimony, and survival', in Shoshana Felman and Dori Laub, M.D., *Testimony: Crises of Witnessing in Literature, Psychoanalysis, and History* (London: Routledge, 1992), 57–74 and 75–92. On this, see also Cathy Caruth, 'Reconstructing the past: Introduction', in *Trauma: Explorations in Memory*, ed. Cathy Caruth (London: Johns Hopkins University Press, 1995), 151–7 (151). As we have seen, Antelme makes it quite clear that his is not a Holocaust testimony; his occasional—and significant—departures from this position are considered further below. I have accordingly sought to understand Antelme's approach to testimony in the light of recent considerations of the question *per se*, without, I hope, encroaching on aspects specific to Holocaust testimony.

2. Lawrence Langer, *Holocaust Testimonies: The Ruins of Memory* (London: Yale University Press, 1991), 2–3.

3. Davis, 'Duras, Antelme', esp. 174.

4. This declaration thus seals the *hic et nunc* quality necessary to testimonial authenticity: on this, see Derrida, *Demeure: Maurice Blanchot* (Paris: Galilée,

1998), 47–9; and Robert Gordon, *Primo Levi's Ordinary Virtues: From Virtue to Ethics* (Oxford: Oxford University Press, 2001), 5.

5. Langer, *Holocaust Testimonies*, 3.

6. Mascolo, *Autour d'un effort de mémoire*, 16–17.

7. Ibid. 17.

8. Ibid. 27, 76.

9. 'Mon cher D., jamais ne reviendront les moments où, tout maigre, je pouvais te dire tant de choses enfouies depuis un an, si riches, si solitaires d'avoir été préservées de l'ennemi et gonflées contre lui' (Mascolo, *Autour d'un effort de mémoire*, 17; see also p. 14, as cited in Ch. 1 above: 'tout dire, c'est là que j'ai vécu mon paradis').

10. Paper on Antelme delivered by Bruno Chaouat to the 54th Kentucky Foreign Language Conference, Univertsity of Kentucky, Lexington, 20 Apr. 2001.

11. Jacques Derrida, *Schibboleth: Pour Paul Celan* (Paris: Galilée, 1986); Felman, 'Education and crisis, or the vicissitudes of teaching', in Felman and Laub, *Testimony*, 1–56 (39); Langer, *Holocaust Testimonies*, 17.

12. 'Nous lisons des livres sur Auschwitz. Le vœu de tous, là-bas, le dernier vœu: sachez ce qui s'est passé, n'oubliez pas, et en même temps jamais vous ne saurez' (Blanchot, *L'Ecriture du désastre*, 131). 'Il *faut*, assurément, il faut inscrire en mots, en images. Pas question d'échapper à la nécessité de représenter. [...] Mais c'est une chose de le faire en vue de sauver la mémoire, une autre d'essayer de réserver le reste, l'oublié inoubliable, dans l'écriture' (Lyotard, *Heidegger et 'les juifs'*, 51–2).

13. Primo Levi, *The Drowned and the Saved* (1986), trans. Raymond Rosenthal, with an Introduction by Paul Bailey (London: Abacus, 1989), 68–9.

14. Antelme's position is developed by Agamben into an equally emphatic refusal, although the referent is shifted specifically to the Holocaust: after citing these lines, Agamben continues: 'To say that Auschwitz is "unsayable" or "incomprehensible" is equivalent to *euphemein*, to adoring in silence, as one does with a god. Regardless of one's intentions, this contributes to its glory' (*Remnants of Auschwitz*, 32–3). This is also the position adopted, *contra* Blanchot, Lyotard and others (although not always addressing the complexities of their models), in Gillian Rose's denunciation of 'Holocaust piety': see her *Mourning Becomes the Law: Philosophy and Representation* (Cambridge: Cambridge University Press, 1996), esp. 43; compare also Jean-Luc Nancy's reference to a 'nimbe de sacralité ou de sainteté' surrounding the invocation of unrepresentability ('La représentation interdite', in *Le Genre humain 36: L'Art et la mémoire des camps: représenter exterminer*, ed. Jean-Luc Nancy (Paris: Seuil, Dec. 2001), 13–39 (14)). With reference primarily to Primo Levi, this debate is very well summarized in Gordon, *Primo Levi's Ordinary Virtues*, 74–9.

15. Compare Rousset, also from 1947: 'Ce livre est construit avec la technique du roman, par méfiance des mots. [...] Toutefois, la fabulation n'a pas de part à ce travail' (David Rousset, *Les Jours de notre mort* (1947), i (Paris: Hachette, 1993), 9); and Semprun's 1994 account of his own initial experience of testimony before liberating soldiers: 'Non pas que l'expérience vécue soit indicible. Elle a été invivable, ce qui est tout autre chose, on le comprendra aisément. Autre chose qui ne concerne pas la forme d'un récit possible, mais sa substance. Non pas son articulation, mais sa densité. Ne parviendront à cette substance, à cette densité que

ceux qui sauront faire de leur témoignage un objet artistique, un espace de création'
(Jorge Semprun, *L'Ecriture ou la vie* (Paris: Gallimard, 1994), 23; the first two of
these sentences also quoted in Gordon, *Primo Levi's Ordinary Virtues*, 75 n. 7).

16. The inextricability of the fictional and the testimonial is addressed by Derrida in
Demeure, esp. 124.

17. Edgar Morin, 'Hommage à Robert Antelme', *Le Monde*, 2 Nov. 1990, 22. See
also *TI*, 266–7.

18. This is the sense of Philippe Lacoue-Labarthe's assertion that, with respect to
L'Espèce humaine, 'on ne pourra jamais dire qu'il s'agit de "littérature"' (*TI*, 161);
the reduction implicit in this attempted separation is discussed in Bruno
Chaouat, 'Ce que chier veut dire (les *ultima excreta* de Robert Antelme)', *Revue
des Sciences Humaines* 261 (Jan. 2001), 147–62 (160–1).

19. For an account of the literary antecedents of Antelme's paratactic style, as part of
a refutation of its supposed 'adequation', see Jacques Rancière, 'S'il y a de
l'irreprésentable', in *Le Genre humain* 36, ed. Nancy, 81–102 (93).

20. The figure of Ulysses—'traveller-storyteller *par excellence*', and emblematic of
heroic return—is of course of great importance to Primo Levi, in whose
writings he assumes a similarly complex status. See Gordon, *Primo Levi's Ordinary
Virtues*, 68–70, 119–20, 248.

21. The scene offers powerful resemblances to that described in the chapter 'The
Canto of Ulysses' in Levi's *If This is a Man*: see Gordon, *Primo Levi's Ordinary
Virtues*, 68–9. Not the least of these resemblances is the precarious establishment
of a moment of connection partly on the basis of a scrap of high culture.

22. Compare Primo Levi's realization that 'the German of the Lager—skeletal,
howled, studded with obscenities and imprecations—was only vaguely related to
the precise, austere language of my chemistry books, and to the melodious,
refined German of Heine's poetry that Clara, a classmate of mine, would recite
to me' (*The Drowned and the Saved*, 75–6).

23. See n. 12 above; and Agamben, *Remnants of Auschwitz*, 39.

24. See n. 16 above.

25. In this sense, Antelme's testimony also offers a more ontologically substantial, but
equally urgent version of the apocalyptic 'Viens!' which, from St. John, has more
recently made its way into Blanchot and Derrida, as a call to the unknowable
future—the non-time of eroded solidarity—in which justice might be done. See
Blanchot, *Le Pas au-delà*, esp. 185; Derrida's essay 'Pas', *Parages*, 19–116; and, on
this quasi-apocalyptic call, John D. Caputo, *The Prayers and Tears of Jacques
Derrida: Religion Without Religion* (Bloomington, IN: Indiana University Press,
1997), esp. 70–80, 96–9, and Hill, *Blanchot: Extreme Contemporary*, 197.

AFTERWORD: '*JA*'

❖

'Rien n'existe plus que l'homme que je ne vois pas.' The closing scene of *L'Espèce humaine* condenses its principal concerns and writing strategies with extraordinary and moving economy. It is punctuated by the refrain, '*Ja*', as Antelme and his unknown Russian neighbour confirm first their respective nationalities, and then, in the text's ringing final lines, their freedom. The divisive, concentrationary logic of their sometime captors is thus refuted in this affirmation of a common humanity—whose inclusiveness is signalled by its affirmation in the language which, most recently, had been that of its attempted denial.

The humanity affirmed is not thematizable, is the shared exposure which defines their common experience; but it does impose, and is marked in, small gestures of non-heroic solidarity: the sharing of a cigarette, a hand on a shoulder. And the exclusive quasi-fraternity of heroic friendship is also refused: shadowy others are there as well. This is not the convergence of the twain, the reunion of twin souls separated ('Parce que c'était lui...'): this is just the man who happens to be next to Antelme when he sits on the bench. It could have been any of them, or none.

The closing, affirmative '*Ja*' is also a demand, of course, challenging the reader to realize the freedom invoked. And the implication of *L'Espèce humaine* is that this realization will have to be double. On the one hand: a radically open friendship for the other person in his irreducible humanity, disclosed most clearly where it is most under assault, in poverty and weakness. On the other: the mobilization of this friendship in specific political action, the necessary, supplementary interventions of the just 'Moi-Sujet'. While this '*Ja*' is a call for justice, then, along the lines of the quasi-apocalyptic 'Viens' of Blanchot and Derrida, it is also folded by Antelme into a specific political context, as the refusal not only of a particular historical violence, but also of the economic and geopolitical regime of which this violence is, for

Antelme, the extreme caricature. In this political dimension, Antelme is, once more, both of his time and of ours. In 1947, a politics is available which seems able to embrace this refusal within its organized oppositional activity. That this appearance proved deceptive is, if anything, only more resonant fifty years on. Speaking to us from the realm of such possible organization, and subsequently finding ways to intervene from beyond its reductive confines, Antelme is perhaps 'out of joint' in the so-called global market—but the articulated solidarity of the refusal he proposes is, potentially, precisely that of the diffuse, under-theorized, and as yet sporadic 'new International' by which this globalization is convulsively being opposed.

Thus, while the popularity of *L'Espèce humaine* may have something to do with its apparently liberal insistence on the indivisibility of humanity, its ethos is in fact compatible with a generalized humanitarian impulse only on very specific grounds. First, that the humanity taken as the basis for this impulse be understood residually, as irreducible exposure, and not betrayed by its positive thematization. Secondly, that the rights of this humanity include those evoked by Antelme in his defence of Bernard Rémy, 'L'homme comme sujet des droits': the right to refuse injustice, and to align oneself un-conditionally with this poor, suffering humanity. And thirdly, therefore: that humanitarian action realize the political radicalism necessary if it is to be other than charitable compensation.

It is easy to mistake unconditional friendship for the subaltern for piety, sentimentalism or idealism. Antelme's political interventions demonstrate the emptiness of such an interpretation. Before the destitute, I find myself subject to a non-negotiable obligation, of course. But in Antelme's analysis, if my response to this obligation is not accompanied by a political challenge to the sources of their destitution, it drifts into the perpetuation and sanctification of what I might imagine myself to be alleviating. If I embrace *L'Espèce humaine*, then, it is not enough for me to feel badly towards the impoverished: writing this in September 2002, for example, at the end of the Johannesburg World Summit on Sustainable Development, I am also bound to protest against the various injustices of disease, poverty and dispossession engendered by the liberal democratic capitalism which thinks of itself as their solution. Of these, I will cite especially, as that which has impinged most during the writing of this study, the doublethink whereby those who celebrate the highly exclusive economic benefits of the global movement of capital simultaneously seek to criminalize the corresponding global movement of those others by whose cheap labour alone these benefits are assured, the new undeserving poor. 'Ce ne sont pas des gens comme nous', indeed.

'Cet ancien "monde véritable"' is still ours.

Yes, indeed.

BIBLIOGRAPHY

❖

1. Works by Antelme

Books

L'Espèce humaine (1947) (Paris: R. Marin, 1949).
L'Espèce humaine, édition revue et corrigée (Paris: Gallimard, 1957).
L'Espèce humaine, édition revue et corrigée (Paris: Gallimard, 'Tel', 1978)
(*EH*).
Textes inédits/Sur 'L'Espèce humaine'/Essais et témoignages (Paris: Gallimard,
1996) (*TI*).

Translations of L'Espèce humaine

Die Gattung Mensch, trans. Dr Roland Schacht (Berlin: Aufbau-Verlag, 1949).
La Specie umana, trans. Ginetta Vittorini (1954; Turin: Einaudi, 1997).
Das Menschengeschlecht, trans. Eugen Helmlé (1987; Frankfurt am Main:
Fischer Taschenbuch, 2001).
The Human Race, trans. Jeffrey Haight and Annie Mahler (Marlboro, VT:
Marlboro Press, 1992).

Articles, letters, declarations

'L'ange au sourire' (n.d.), *TI*, 15–16.
'Poèmes' (1944), *TI*, 52–7: 'Le train' (53); 'Monologue du sang' (54–5); 'Les
deux' (56); 'Forêt' (56–7).
Letter to Dionys Mascolo (1945), in Mascolo, *Autour d'un effort de mémoire*,
13–18 and 91–5.
'Vengeance?' (1945), *TI*, 17–24.
'De l'Allemagne nazie et des Allemands' (1946), *Lignes*, 3 (N.S.) (Paris: Léo
Scheer, Oct. 2000), 179–82.
'On m'a volé mon pain' (1947), *TI*, 58–66. (Extract from original edition of
L'Espèce humaine, removed from 1957 edition.)
'Pauvre — prolétaire — déporté' (1948), *TI*, 25–32.
'Rapport au Cercle des critiques sur les questions de la littérature et de
l'esthétique' (co-authored with Dionys Mascolo) (1948), *Lignes* 33: *Avec
Dionys Mascolo*, 25–39.

'Témoignage du camp et poésie' (1948), *TI*, 44–8.
'J'accepte sous conditions (Réponse à David Rousset)' (1949), *Lignes* 3 (N.S.)
(Paris: Léo Scheer, Oct. 2000), 187–91.
'Les principes à l'épreuve' (1958), *TI*, 33–8.
'En vue de la défaite américaine: appel international pour une rupture'
(1967), *Lignes* 33: *Avec Dionys Mascolo*, 99–101.
'L'homme comme sujet des droits' (1974), *TI*, 39–43.
'Sur *L'Ecriture du désastre* de Maurice Blanchot' (1981), *TI*, 67–8.

2. Secondary Materials

ADLER, LAURE, *Marguerite Duras* (Paris: Gallimard, 1998).
ADORNO, THEODOR W., *Negative Dialectics* (1966), trans. E. B. Ashton
(London: Routledge, 1996).
AGAMBEN, GIORGIO, *Homo Sacer: Sovereign Power and Bare Life* (1995), trans.
Daniel Heller-Roazen (Stanford, CA: Stanford University Press, 1998).
—— *Remnants of Auschwitz: The Witness and the Archive*, trans. Daniel Heller-
Roazen (New York: Zone Books, 1999).
AMÉRY, JEAN, *At the Mind's Limits: Contemplations by a Survivor on Auschwitz
and its Realities* (1966), trans. Sidney Rosenfeld and Stella P. Rosenfeld
(Bloomington, IN: Indiana University Press, 1980).
—— *Radical Humanism: Selected Essays*, ed. and trans. Sidney Rosenfeld and
Stella P. Rosenfeld (Bloomington, IN: Indiana University Press, 1984).
ANTELME, MONIQUE, 'Jorge Semprun n'a pas dit la vérité', *Le Monde*, 8 July
1998, 11.
ASSOULINE, PIERRE, *Gaston Gallimard, un demi-siècle d'édition française* (1984)
(Paris: Seuil, 'Points', 1996).
AUDIBERTI, JACQUES, *L'Abhumanisme* (Paris: Gallimard, 1955).
DE BAECQUE, ANTOINE, and JOUSSE, THIERRY, 'Jacques Derrida: le cinéma
et ses fantômes', *Cahiers du cinéma* 556 (Apr. 2001), 74–85.
BEARDSWORTH, RICHARD, *Derrida and the Political* (London: Routledge,
1996).
BELLOS, DAVID, *Georges Perec: A Life in Words* (London: Harvill, 1993).
BENSLAMA, FETHI, 'Le propre de l'homme', *TI*, 91–105.
—— 'La représentation et l'impossible', in *Le Genre humain* 36: *L'Art et la
mémoire des camps*, ed. Jean-Luc Nancy, 59–80.
BETTELHEIM, BRUNO, *Surviving, and Other Essays* (London: Thames and
Hudson, 1979).
BIDENT, CHRISTOPHE, *Maurice Blanchot: Partenaire invisible* (Seyssel: Champ
Vallon, 1998).
BLANCHOT, MAURICE, *La Part du feu* (Paris: Gallimard, 1949).
—— *Le Dernier Homme* (1957), nouvelle version (1977) (Paris: Gallimard,
L'Imaginaire, 2001).

—— *L'Amitié* (Paris: Gallimard, 1971).

—— *Le Pas au-delà* (Paris: Gallimard, 1973).

—— *L'Ecriture du désastre* (Paris: Gallimard, 1980).

—— 'Dans la nuit surveillée', *TI*, 71–6.

—— 'L'espèce humaine' (1962), in *L'Entretien infini* (Paris: Gallimard, 1969), 191–200

—— 'Exergue', *TI*, 252 (extract from Blanchot, 'Pré-texte: Pour l'amitié').

—— 'Pré-texte: Pour l'amitié', in Mascolo, *A la recherche d'un communisme de pensée*, 5–16 (repr. as Blanchot, *Pour l'amitié* (Paris: Fourbis, 1996)).

BONSAVER, GUIDO, *Elio Vittorini: The Writer and the Written* (Leeds: Northern Universities Press, 2000).

DU BOUCHET, ANDRÉ, 'Une lettre d'André du Bouchet', *TI*, 248.

CAMUS, ALBERT, *Lettres à un ami allemand* (1943–5) (Paris: Gallimard, Folio, 1991).

—— *L'Homme révolté* (1951) (Paris: Gallimard, Folio, 1985).

CAPUTO, JOHN D., *The Prayers and Tears of Jacques Derrida: Religion Without Religion* (Bloomington, IN: Indiana University Press, 1997).

CARUTH, CATHY (ed.), *Trauma: Explorations in Memory* (London: Johns Hopkins University Press, 1995).

CAYROL, JEAN, *Nuit et brouillard* suivi de: *De la mort à la vie* (Paris: Fayard, 1997).

CHAOUAT, BRUNO, '"La mort ne recèle pas tant de mystère": Robert Antelme's defaced humanism', *L'Esprit Créateur* 40/1 (Spring 2000), 88–99.

—— 'Ce que chier veut dire (les *ultima excreta* de Robert Antelme)', *Revue des Sciences Humaines* 261 (Jan.–Mar. 2001), 147–62.

—— 'Robert Antelme's defaced humanism', paper delivered at the 54th Kentucky Foreign Language Conference, University of Kentucky, Lexington, 20 Apr. 2001.

CRITCHLEY, SIMON, *Ethics—Politics—Subjectivity: Essays on Derrida, Levinas and Contemporary French Thought* (London: Verso, 1999).

CROWLEY, MARTIN, *Duras, Writing, and the Ethical: Making the Broken Whole* (Oxford: Oxford University Press, 2000).

—— '"Il n'y a qu'une espèce humaine": Between Duras and Antelme', in *The Holocaust and the Text: Speaking the Unspeakable*, ed. Andrew Leak and George Paizis (Basingstoke: Macmillan, 2000), 174–92.

—— 'Remaining human: Robert Antelme's *L'Espèce humaine*', *French Studies* 56/4 (Oct. 2002), 35–46.

DAIX, PIERRE, *Les Hérétiques du P.C.F.* (Paris: Robert Laffont, 1980).

—— 'Pierre Daix, matricule 59.807 à Mauthausen répond à David Rousset', *Les Lettres françaises*, 17 Nov. 1949, 1, 4.

DAVIS, COLIN, 'Duras, Antelme, and the ethics of writing', *Comparative Literature Studies* 34/2 (1997), 169–83.

DAVIS, COLIN, 'Antelme, Levinas, and the shock of the other', paper delivered at the 54th Kentucky Foreign Language Conference, University of Kentucky, Lexington, 20 April 2001. (To be published as 'Antelme, Renoir, Levinas, and the shock of the other', *French Cultural Studies*, forthcoming.)

—— 'David Rousset', in *Holocaust Literature*, ed. S. Lillian Kremer (London: Routledge, forthcoming).

—— 'Robert Antelme', in *Holocaust Literature*, ed. S. Lillian Kremer (London: Routledge, forthcoming).

DELBO, CHARLOTTE, *Auschwitz et après*, i: *Aucun de nous ne reviendra* (Paris: Minuit, 1970).

—— *Auschwitz et après*, ii: *Une connaissance inutile* (Paris: Minuit, 1970).

—— *Auschwitz et après*, iii: *Mesure de nos jours* (Paris: Minuit, 1971).

DERRIDA, JACQUES, *Parages* (Paris: Galilée, 1986).

—— *Schibboleth: Pour Paul Celan* (Paris: Galilée, 1986).

—— *Feu la cendre* (1987) (Paris: Editions des Femmes, 1998).

—— *Spectres de Marx* (Paris: Galilée, 1993).

—— *Politiques de l'amitié* (Paris: Galilée, 1994).

—— *Demeure: Maurice Blanchot* (Paris: Galilée, 1998).

—— 'Les fins de l'homme' (1968), in *Marges de la philosophie* (Paris: Minuit, 1972), 129–64.

—— 'Signature événement contexte' (1971), in *Marges de la philosophie* (Paris: Minuit, 1972), 365–93.

DES PRES, TERRENCE, *The Survivor: An Anatomy of Life in the Death Camps* (New York, NY: Oxford University Press, 1976).

DOBBELS, DANIEL, 'La veine du corps', *TI*, 234–47.

DOMINIQUE, FRANÇOIS, 'Nous sommes libres ...', *TI*, 204–20.

DURAS, MARGUERITE, *La Maladie de la mort* (Paris: Minuit, 1981).

—— 'Le rêve heureux du crime', in *Outside* (1981; Paris: P.O.L., 1984), 283–7.

FAYE, JEAN-PIERRE, 'Les trous du visage', *TI*, 88–90.

FELMAN, SHOSHANA, and LAUB, DORI, *Testimony: Crises of Witnessing in Literature, Psychoanalysis, and History* (London: Routledge, 1992).

GLOVER, JONATHAN, *Humanity: A Moral History of the Twentieth Century* (London: Jonathan Cape, 1999).

GORDON, ROBERT, *Primo Levi's Ordinary Virtues: From Testimony to Ethics* (Oxford: Oxford University Press, 2001).

'GRATIEN, JEAN' (DIONYS MASCOLO), and MORIN, EDGAR, 'Une interview d'Elio Vittorini', *Les Lettres françaises*, 27 June 1947, 1, 7.

HEGEL, G. W. F., *The Phenomenology of Mind* (1807), trans. with introduction and notes by J. B. Baillie, 2nd edn. (London: George Allen & Unwin, 1951).

HILL, LESLIE, *Blanchot: Extreme Contemporary* (London: Routledge, 1997).

—— *Bataille, Klossowski, Blanchot: Writing at the Limit* (Oxford: Oxford University Press, 2001).

JAMES, IAN, *Pierre Klossowski: The Persistence of a Name* (Oxford: Legenda, 2000).

JARON, STEVEN, 'Autobiography and the Holocaust: An examination of the liminal generation in France', *French Studies* 56/2 (Apr. 2002), 207–19.

KAEPPELIN, OLIVIER, 'L'ultime chose commune que nous possédions', *TI*, 230–3.

KAPLAN, LESLIE, 'Penser la mort', *TI*, 106–13.

KLEIN, NAOMI, *No Logo* (2000; London: Flamingo, 2001).

KOFMAN, SARAH, *Paroles suffoquées* (Paris: Galilée, 1986).

—— 'Les "mains" d'Antelme (Post-scriptum à *Paroles suffoquées*)', *TI*, 147–51.

KOJÈVE, ALEXANDRE, *Introduction à la lecture de Hegel: Leçons sur la 'Phénoménologie de l'esprit'*, réunies et publiées par Raymond Queneau (Paris: Gallimard, 1947).

LACAPRA, DOMINIC, *Representing the Holocaust: History, Theory, Trauma* (Ithaca, NY: Cornell University Press, 1994).

LACOUE-LABARTHE, PHILIPPE, 'Moscou, 1er décembre...', *TI*, 160–1.

LANGER, LAWRENCE L., *Holocaust Testimonies: The Ruins of Memory* (London: Yale University Press, 1991).

LAPORTE, ROGER, 'L'Interruption — l'interminable', *TI*, 145–6.

LEJEUNE, PHILIPPE, *La Mémoire et l'oblique: Georges Perec autobiographe* (Paris: P.O.L., 1991).

LEPAPE, PIERRE, 'Mort de l'écrivain Robert Antelme', *Le Monde*, 30 Oct. 1990, 36.

LEVI, PRIMO, *If This is a Man* (1947) and *The Truce* (1963), trans. Stuart Woolf, with an introduction by Paul Bailey and afterword by the author (London: Abacus, 1987).

—— *Moments of Reprieve* (1981), trans. Ruth Feldman (London: Michael Joseph, 1986).

—— *The Drowned and the Saved* (1986), trans. Raymond Rosenthal, with introduction by Paul Bailey (London: Abacus, 1989).

Lignes 33: *Avec Dionys Mascolo* (Paris: Hazan, 1998).

Lignes 2 (N.S.): *David Rousset* (Paris: Léo Scheer, May 2000).

LINGIS, ALPHONSO, *The Community of Those Who Have Nothing in Common* (Bloomington, IN: Indiana University Press, 1994).

LYOTARD, JEAN-FRANÇOIS, *Heidegger et 'les juifs'* (Paris: Galilée, 1988).

—— 'Discussions, ou: phraser "après Auschwitz"', in *Les Fins de l'homme: à partir du travail de Jacques Derrida* (Colloque de Cerisy, 23 juillet–2 août 1980), ed. Philippe Lacoue-Labarthe and Jean-Luc Nancy (Paris: Galilée, 1981), 283–315.

MARMANDE, FRANCIS, 'La vérité telle qu'elle...', *TI*, 191–9.

MARX, KARL, 'The Economic and Philosophical Manuscripts of 1844', in *Karl Marx: A Reader*, ed. Jon Elster (Cambridge: Cambridge University Press, 1986), 35–47.

MARX, KARL, *Manuscrits de 1844*, trans. Jacques-Pierre Gougeon, with introduction, notes, bibliography and chronology by Jean Salem (Paris: Flammarion, 1996).

—— *Le 18 brumaire de Louis Bonaparte* (1852) (Paris: Mille et une nuits, 1997).

MASCOLO, DIONYS, *Autour d'un effort de mémoire: Sur une lettre de Robert Antelme* (Paris: Maurice Nadeau, 1987).

—— *A la recherche d'un communisme de pensée* (Paris: Fourbis, 1993).

—— 'Appel du comité d'action contre la poursuite de la guerre en Afrique du Nord' (1955), *Lignes* 33: *Avec Dionys Mascolo*, 65–7.

MINIÈRE, CLAUDE, 'La convenance', *TI*, 200–3.

MORIN, EDGAR, *Autocritique* (Paris: Seuil, 1970).

—— 'Hommage à Robert Antelme', *Le Monde*, 2 Nov. 1990, 22.

NADEAU, MAURICE, '*Les Jours de notre mort* comme œuvre littéraire', *Lignes* 2 (N.S.): *David Rousset*, 82–9.

NANCY, JEAN-LUC, *La Communauté désœuvrée* (1986), nouvelle édition revue et augmentée (Paris: Christian Bourgois, 1999).

—— 'Les deux phrases de Robert Antelme', *TI*, 140–1.

—— 'La représentation interdite', in *Le Genre humain* 36: *L'Art et la mémoire des camps*, ed. Jean-Luc Nancy, 13–39.

—— (ed.), *Le Genre humain* 36: *L'Art et la mémoire des camps: représenter exterminer* (Paris: Seuil, Dec. 2001).

NORMAN, RICHARD, *Hegel's Phenomenology: A Philosophical Introduction* (London: Sussex University Press/Chatto & Windus, 1976).

PEREC, GEORGES, *L.G. Une aventure des années soixante* (Paris: Seuil, 1992).

—— 'Robert Antelme ou la vérité de la littérature' (1963), *TI*, 173–90. (Also in Perec, *L.G. Une aventure des années soixante*, 87–114.)

POTTER, JOY HAMBUECHEN, *Elio Vittorini* (Boston, MA: Twayne, 1979).

RABAN, CLAUDE, 'Se soulever contre ce qui est là…', *TI*, 120–39.

RABINOVITCH, GÉRARD, 'Dans un monde médusé', *TI*, 162–72.

RANCIÈRE, JACQUES, 'S'il y a de l'irreprésentable', in *Le Genre humain* 36: *L'Art et la mémoire des camps*, ed. Jean-Luc Nancy, 81–102.

REVAULT D'ALLONNES, MYRIAM, 'L'homme nu', *TI*, 142–4.

ROBSON, KATHRYN, 'Writing Wounds: The Inscription of Trauma in Post-1968 French Women's Life-Writing', Ph.D. thesis (Cambridge, 2001).

ROSE, GILLIAN, *Mourning Becomes the Law: Philosophy and Representation* (Cambridge: Cambridge University Press, 1996).

ROUDAUT, JEAN, 'L'espèce humaine', *TI*, 221–9.

ROUSSET, DAVID, *Les Jours de notre mort* (1947), 2 vols. (Paris: Hachette, 1993).

—— *L'Univers concentrationnaire* (1945) (Paris: Hachette Littératures, 1998).

—— 'Au secours des déportés dans les camps soviétiques: Un appel aux anciens déportés des camps nazis' (1949), *Lignes* 2 (N.S.): *David Rousset*, 143–60.

—— 'Lettre à Robert Antelme' *Lignes*, 3 (N.S.) (Paris: Léo Scheer, Oct. 2000), 183–6.

ROY, CLAUDE, *Nous* (1972) (Paris: Gallimard, Folio, 1980).

—— 'Post-scriptum', *TI*, 273–5.

SADE, DONATIEN ALPHONSE FRANÇOIS, MARQUIS DE, *Œuvres complètes du Marquis de Sade*, édition définitive, 16 vols. (Paris: Au Cercle du livre précieux, 1966–7).

SAEZ, JEAN-PIERRE, 'Autour de Robert Antelme', *TI*, 252–72.

SEMPRUN, JORGE, *Le Grand Voyage* (1963) (Paris: Gallimard, Folio, 2000).

—— *Quel beau dimanche!* (Paris: Grasset, 1980).

—— *L'Ecriture ou la vie* (Paris: Gallimard, 1994).

—— 'Non, je n'ai pas "dénoncé" Marguerite Duras', *Le Monde*, 26 June 1998, 16.

SPRINKER, MICHAEL (ed.), *Ghostly Demarcations: A Symposium on Jacques Derrida's 'Specters of Marx'* (London: Verso, 1999).

STIEGLER, BERND, *Die Aufgabe des Namens: zur Funktion der Eigennamen in der Literatur des 20. Jahrhunderts* (Munich: Wilhelm Fink, 1994).

STONE, DAN, 'Perec's Antelme', *French Cultural Studies* 10/2 (June 1999), 161–72.

STREIFF, GÉRARD, *Procès stalinien à Saint-Germain-des-Prés* (Paris: Syllepse, 1999).

SURYA, MICHEL, 'Une absence d'issue', *TI*, 114–19. (Repr. as 'Une littérature de l'irrémédiable (le "tout dire" sans issue de Robert Antelme)', in Michel Surya, *Matériologies*, i: *L'Imprécation littéraire* (Tours: Farrago, 1999), 163–70.)

'Témoignages', *TI*, 276–96.

VITTORINI, ELIO, *Conversation en Sicile* (1937–8), trans. Michel Arnaud (Paris: Gallimard, L'Imaginaire, 2001).

—— *Les Hommes et les autres* (1945), trans. Michel Arnaud (Paris: Gallimard, L'Etrangère, 1992).

WIEVIORKA, ANNETTE, *Déportation et génocide* (Paris: Plon, 1992).

WILSON, EMMA, *Memory and Survival: The French Cinema of Krzysztof Kieślowski* (Oxford: Legenda, 2000).

ŽIŽEK, SLAVOJ, *The Sublime Object of Ideology* (London: Verso, 1989).

INDEX

❖

SOCIETY FOR FRENCH STUDIES

The Society for French Studies, the oldest and leading learned association for French studies in the UK and Ireland, promotes teaching and research in French studies in higher education. Membership is open to all interested; postgraduates and lecturers in the first three years of employment pay a reduced subscription. The Society's activities include:

• Editing *French Studies*, a quarterly journal (articles in French literary and cultural studies and a wide range of book reviews) and its companion *French Studies Bulletin* (short articles, information from societies, calls for papers, etc.), both sent free to members

• Maintaining the online database of research projects in the UK and Ireland, *Current Research in French Studies* (at www.sfs.ac.uk), and compiling the annual *Directory of Postgraduate Research Students of French*, free to members

• Hosting an annual conference with distinguished speakers and varied workshops

• Promoting research through: conference and seminar grants; the R. H. Gapper annual book and essay prizes; joint publication of Legenda Research Monographs in French Studies (with 33% discount to SFS members); postgraduate support via subsidized membership fees and conference expenses, an electronic bulletin board and other services

• Maintaining a website with rapidly expanding resources: **www.sfs.ac.uk**

Membership enquiries: Dr Gill Rye
Institute of Romance Studies, University of London
Senate House, Malet Street, London WC1E 7HU, UK
membership@sfs.ac.uk

The Society for French Studies is charity no. 1078038 and is a company, limited by guarantee, registered in England and Wales, no. 3801778, whose registered office is the Taylor Institution, Oxford OX1 3NA.